A STUDENT'S

MODELS
FOR
WRITERS

A STUDENT'S COMPANION FOR
MODELS FOR WRITERS

Short Essays for Composition

FOURTEENTH EDITION

Elizabeth Catanese
Community College of Philadelphia

with contributions from
Carolyn Lengel
Andrew B. Preslar
Lamar State College — Orange

bedford/st.martin's
Macmillan Learning
Boston | New York

Vice President: Leasa Burton
Program Director, English: Stacey Purviance
Senior Program Manager: John E. Sullivan III
Director of Content Development: Jane Knetzger
Development Editor: Will Stonefield
Assistant Editor: Paola García-Muñiz
Director of Media Editorial: Adam Whitehurst
Associate Media Editor: Daniel Johnson
Executive Marketing Manager: Joy Fisher Williams
Senior Director, Content Management Enhancement: Tracey Kuehn
Senior Managing Editor: Michael Granger
Senior Manager of Publishing Services: Andrea Cava
Senior Content Project Manager: Pamela Lawson
Lead Digital Asset Archivist and Senior Workflow Project Manager: Jennifer Wetzel
Production Coordinator: Brianna Lester
Director of Design, Content Management: Diana Blume
Cover Design: William Boardman
Cover Image: Jules Kitano_Getty Images
Director of Digital Production: Keri deManigold
Advanced Media Project Manager: Rand Thomas
Project Management: Lumina Datamatics, Inc.
Project Manager: Anandan Bommen
Editorial Services: Lumina Datamatics, Inc.
Composition: Lumina Datamatics, Inc.
Printing and Binding: LSC Communications

Copyright © 2021 by Bedford/St. Martin's. No part of this book may be reproduced, stored in a retrieval system, or transmitted in any form or by any means, electronic, mechanical, photocopying, recording, or otherwise, except as may be permitted by law or expressly permitted in writing by the Publisher.

Library of Congress Control Number: 2020937127
ISBN 978-1-319-32595-4

Printed in the United States of America.
1 2 3 4 5 6   25 24 23 22 21 20

For information, write: Bedford/St. Martin's, 75 Arlington Street, Boston, MA 02116

INTRODUCTION

A *Student's Companion for Models for Writers* reinforces the most foundational elements in academic writing. While recognizing and respecting your abilities, this supplement breaks down the steps necessary to excel in college writing, build confidence, tackle time management, and write ethically; it provides additional activities to help you draft, revise, and edit college-level work; and it provides sentence guides for academic writing, as well as editing practice. This companion, meant to supplement the coverage in *Models for Writers*, gives you additional support for your composition class. For your instructor, it is an ideal solution for accelerated learning programs or corequisite courses, while the deep integration with *Models for Writers* makes it an ideal resource for any instructor who wants students to build a strong foundation in academic writing.

PART ONE: SUCCEEDING IN COLLEGE

Part One addresses topics that are critical to your success: confidence building, time management, and ethical and responsible writing. This coverage can be a handy reference outside of class.

PART TWO: WRITING ACTIVITIES

Part Two of this workbook begins with an overview of the patterns of organization covered in *Models for Writers*:

- Illustration
- Narration

- Description
- Process analysis
- Definition
- Division and classification
- Comparison and contrast
- Cause and effect
- Argument

Chapter 4 offers activities students can use to craft paragraphs in each of these patterns, so they can get a sense of how each pattern of organization works.

Since students learn best by doing, subsequent chapters in Part Two offer step-by-step activities, with loads of sentence guides. Each of these activities is designed to help students devise a topic, assess their audience, craft a thesis, develop their ideas fully, and revise and edit their drafts. Also included in each of these chapters is a rubric that instructors and students can use to make the expectations of college writing clear for assignments in each of these patterns. The activities and rubrics in Part Two can be used in a workshop-oriented class or be assigned as homework to encourage students to think, write, and revise critically and deeply.

PART THREE: ADDITIONAL TOOLS FOR PRACTICE

Part Three begins with sentence guides that help you learn to present information and ideas to others, present your own views, and then put the pieces together to write an effective academic essay. If you need additional help, you can also get practice with editing sentences and paragraphs, reviewing the parts of speech, writing correct sentences, managing punctuation, mechanics, spelling, and more. You can choose the areas where you need to grow, or your instructor can point you to activities based on the specific struggles that emerge in your papers.

The overall goal for this workbook is to help you become an increasingly engaged, professional, and happy writer. Have a wonderful semester!

Elizabeth Catanese
Assistant Professor, English
Community College of Philadelphia

CONTENTS

INTRODUCTION   v

PART ONE
SUCCEEDING IN COLLEGE   1

1   BUILDING YOUR CONFIDENCE   3

    NOT FEELING CONFIDENT   4
    IDENTIFYING STRENGTHS AND SETTING GOALS   4
    The Confidence Checklist   5
    LEARNING FROM YOUR EXPERIENCES AND CHOICES   6
    TAKING RISKS   6
    Taking Risks in the Classroom • Speaking Up in Class
    Exercise: Questions and Answers
    EXAMINING EMOTIONS   8
    Exercise: What Makes a Success?   8
    BEING PERSISTENT   8
    Assertiveness Check-Up   9
    BEING ASSERTIVE   9
    DEVELOPING A NETWORK   10
    ADVICE FROM OTHER STUDENTS   11
    Tips for Confidence-Building   11

2   MANAGING YOUR TIME   13

    THE CASE FOR TIME MANAGEMENT   13
    TAKING CHARGE OF YOUR TIME   14
    Setting Goals • Knowing Your Priorities

Control Factor: Know What You Can and Can't Control   17
What You Can Control   17
What You Can't Control   17
FOUR TIME-WASTING HABITS TO AVOID   18
1. Procrastinating • 2. Overextending Yourself • 3. Losing Your Focus • 4. Running Late
TWO INDISPENSABLE TOOLS TO KEEP YOU ON TRACK   20
A Planner or Calendar • A To-Do List
ADVICE FROM OTHER STUDENTS   22
Easy Ways to Maximize Your Time   23

3   WRITING ETHICALLY AND RESPONSIBLY   25

DEFINING "CHEATING"   25
THE CHEATING PROBLEM   26
WHY YOU SHOULDN'T CHEAT   27
WHY IT'S EASY TO GET CAUGHT   27
HOW *NOT* TO CHEAT: TEN ESSENTIAL TIPS   27
The Penalties for Cheating   28
THE RULES OF PARAPHRASING   30

PART TWO
WRITING ACTIVITIES   33

4   PATTERNS OF ORGANIZATION   35

PREWRITING ACTIVITIES   35
Illustration • Narration • Description • Process Analysis • Definition • Division and Classification • Comparison and Contrast • Cause and Effect • Argument
ESSAY ORGANIZATION ACTIVITIES   40

5   ILLUSTRATION   43

PREWRITING ACTIVITIES   43
THESIS ACTIVITIES   47
DRAFTING ACTIVITIES   49
FEEDBACK ACTIVITIES   52
Rubric for Assessing Illustration Essays   54
REVISION AND EDITING ACTIVITIES   57

6   NARRATION   59

    PREWRITING ACTIVITIES   59
    THESIS ACTIVITIES   64
    DRAFTING ACTIVITIES   66
    FEEDBACK ACTIVITIES   70
    Rubric for Assessing Narration Essays   71
    REVISION AND EDITING ACTIVITIES   76

7   DESCRIPTION   78

    PREWRITING ACTIVITIES   78
    THESIS ACTIVITIES   82
    DRAFTING ACTIVITIES   84
    FEEDBACK ACTIVITIES   88
    Rubric for Assessing Description Essays   90
    REVISION AND EDITING ACTIVITIES   95

8   PROCESS ANALYSIS   97

    PREWRITING ACTIVITIES   97
    THESIS ACTIVITIES   101
    DRAFTING ACTIVITIES   103
    FEEDBACK ACTIVITIES   106
    Rubric for Assessing Process Analysis Essays   108
    REVISION AND EDITING ACTIVITIES   112

9   DEFINITION   114

    PREWRITING ACTIVITIES   114
    THESIS ACTIVITIES   118
    DRAFTING ACTIVITIES   120
    FEEDBACK ACTIVITIES   123
    Rubric for Assessing Definition Essays   125
    REVISION AND EDITING ACTIVITIES   129

10   DIVISION AND CLASSIFICATION   132

    PREWRITING ACTIVITIES   132
    THESIS ACTIVITIES   136
    DRAFTING ACTIVITIES   138

FEEDBACK ACTIVITIES 142
Rubric for Assessing Division and Classification Essays 143
REVISION AND EDITING ACTIVITIES 148

11 COMPARISON AND CONTRAST 150

PREWRITING ACTIVITIES 150
THESIS ACTIVITIES 154
DRAFTING ACTIVITIES 155
FEEDBACK ACTIVITIES 159
Rubric for Assessing Comparison-and-Contrast Essays 161
REVISION AND EDITING ACTIVITIES 165

12 CAUSE AND EFFECT 167

PREWRITING ACTIVITIES 167
THESIS ACTIVITIES 171
DRAFTING ACTIVITIES 173
FEEDBACK ACTIVITIES 177
Rubric for Assessing Cause-and-Effect Essays 179
REVISION AND EDITING ACTIVITIES 183

13 ARGUMENT 185

PREWRITING ACTIVITIES 185
THESIS ACTIVITIES 190
DRAFTING ACTIVITIES 191
FEEDBACK ACTIVITIES 195
Rubric for Assessing Argument Essays 196
REVISION AND EDITING ACTIVITIES 201

PART THREE
ADDITIONAL TOOLS FOR PRACTICE 205

14 SENTENCE GUIDES FOR ACADEMIC WRITERS 207

ACADEMIC WRITERS PRESENT INFORMATION AND OTHERS' VIEWS 208
Presenting What Is Known or Assumed • Presenting Others' Views • Presenting Direct Quotations • Presenting Alternative Views

ACADEMIC WRITERS PRESENT THEIR OWN VIEWS   211
Presenting Your Own Views: Agreement and Extension • Presenting Your Own Views: Queries and Skepticism • Presenting Your Own Views: Disagreement or Correction • Presenting and Countering Objections to Your Argument

ACADEMIC WRITERS PERSUADE BY PUTTING IT ALL TOGETHER   214
Presenting Stakeholders • Presenting the "So What" • Presenting the Players and Positions in a Debate • Using Appropriate Signal Verbs

15 WRITING GRAMMATICALLY CORRECT SENTENCES   218

CORRECTING SENTENCE BOUNDARY ISSUES   218
Identifying Subjects and Verbs • The Implied You • Correcting Sentence Fragments • Your Sentences • Run-Ons and Fragments in Context • Run-Ons and Fragments in the Real World • Pronouns • Pronouns in Your Work

16 WRITING CLEAR SENTENCES IN A THOUGHTFUL STYLE   225

SENTENCE COMBINATION   225
SENTENCE COMBINATION IN YOUR WORK   227
SUBJECT/VERB AGREEMENT   227
CONJUGATIONS   228
VOCABULARY DEVELOPMENT IN PAPERS   230
SPECIFICITY AND PRECISION OF LANGUAGE   231
DESCRIPTION AND PARAGRAPH EXPANSION   232
TRANSITIONS   234
RESEARCH SKILLS   236
Paraphrasing • Paraphrasing Steps • Quotation Sandwich • Paragraph Incorporating Quotation

17 ACTIVITIES FOR IMPROVING YOUR WRITING   239

REVISION ACTIVITY   239
PEER REVIEW ACTIVITY   240
THESIS STATEMENT ACTIVITY   240
TOPIC SENTENCES ACTIVITY   241
USING MODELS ACTIVITY   241

A STUDENT'S COMPANION FOR

MODELS FOR WRITERS

PART ONE

SUCCEEDING IN COLLEGE

1 Building Your Confidence   3

2 Managing Your Time   13

3 Writing Ethically and Responsibly   25

1

BUILDING YOUR CONFIDENCE

Confidence can help drive and shape your experiences as a student, performer, athlete, employee, parent, and the many other roles you play in your life. True confidence is often defined as having a positive and realistic belief about yourself and your talents and traits. *Assertive, optimistic, eager, proud, independent, trustworthy,* and *mature* are some of the many terms associated with someone who has true confidence. Conversely, a lack of confidence can result in a poor performance in those same roles.

Here are just a few reasons to develop confidence:

- **Confidence helps sell who you are.** Knowledge, skills, and experience are necessary and important. If you do not possess and project an air of confidence, others may not realize you have these qualities.
- **Confidence reassures others.** It can create trust in the people in your life, whether they are your peers, classmates, coworkers, or loved ones.

This guide explores the role that confidence plays in everyday success and offers strategies on building your confidence levels around all of the roles you play in your life.

NOT FEELING CONFIDENT

Have you had any trouble maintaining your confidence since you started college? It may surprise you to learn that you are not the only first-year student who feels this way. Many students who enter college for the first time feel just like you do: not very certain of all that lies ahead and unsure how to deal with a number of challenges, both in and out of the classroom. Below are just a few steps you can take to help to develop more confidence:

- **Take a strengths inventory.** Make a list of what you're good at.
- **Set measurable, attainable goals.** Ask yourself what you want to accomplish in the next week, month, or year, and then break those goals up into smaller, short-term goals.
- **Take responsibility for your actions.** Make a consistent effort to learn from your experiences (the good and the bad) and own your choices.
- **Dare to take intellectual risks.** Question assumptions, and ask yourself if the things you believe to be true actually are.
- **Examine and acknowledge feelings.** When something bothers you, ask why.
- **Take charge and be persistent.** Remember, luck is 99 percent perseverance.
- **Assert yourself.** When you want something, you've got to ask.
- **Remember, you're not alone.** Identify individuals who exhibit confidence, and make a strong effort to model the types of behavior that make the greatest impression on you.
- **Believe in yourself.**

IDENTIFYING STRENGTHS AND SETTING GOALS

Why not start building your confidence by reminding yourself what you are good at? You can start with this simple, yet effective, activity:

Make a list of what you believe are your strongest skills and qualities. Take the time to think deeply and honestly about this exercise before you start. Another way to do this is to ask yourself: "When I feel like I am at my best, what am I doing?" Continue performing those activities to create an increased sense of confidence.

Long-term goals vs. short-term goals: How do they differ? A crucial part of developing, building, and maintaining your confidence is to set long- and short-term goals that you can reach and that are able to meet your expectations. Think of long-term goals as the final product and short-term goals as the steps along the way. For example, if you were to write a ten-chapter novel, you'd have ten short-term goals (write a chapter) and one long-term goal (write a novel).

THE CONFIDENCE CHECKLIST

Before examining a series of meaningful steps you can take to build confidence, let's start with the following confidence checklist. How would you respond to the following statements? Be as completely truthful and objective as you can be.

	Yes	No
I believe I know what is best for me.	☐	☐
I feel I am a genuine person.	☐	☐
I am extremely tolerant of others in my life.	☐	☐
I am consistent—I do as I say.	☐	☐
I avoid procrastinating.	☐	☐
I take an active role in classroom discussions.	☐	☐
I have an inner voice that guides my decisions.	☐	☐
I maintain good eye contact and tone of voice when speaking.	☐	☐
I often doubt myself.	☐	☐
I am able to handle constructive criticism.	☐	☐
I have difficulty trusting others.	☐	☐
I prefer being alone than being with groups of people.	☐	☐
I would describe myself as an outgoing and assertive individual.	☐	☐
I feel I am capable of assessing my true capabilities.	☐	☐
I am an optimistic person by nature.	☐	☐

If you answered "no" to more than half of the statements, your level of confidence is likely not where you want it to be—and you're probably not alone! Keep reading for some proven strategies to boost your confidence.

Now it's your turn.

- Select one goal you would like to achieve in the next month. Be specific about what that goal is.

- Now identify two or three effective actions you will take to obtain this goal. Once again, be specific and include a time frame for performing these actions.
- Think of one possible barrier that might prevent you from reaching this goal.
- Now consider one action you will take to overcome this barrier. Be sure to detail what this action will be.
- Last, predict what you honestly believe will be your degree of success in eventually achieving this goal.

> **TIP**
>
> So how does setting goals help build confidence? Think about it this way: If you set up a series of short-term goals you know you can achieve, aren't you going to feel more confident each time you check off one of those goals? Even better, aren't you going to feel like a rock star by the time you achieve your ultimate long-term goal? There is nothing that builds more confidence than seeing hard work pay off.

LEARNING FROM YOUR EXPERIENCES AND CHOICES

Wisdom can often be gained through both good and bad experiences and through the outcomes of the choices we make. If you can accept that you are ultimately the one responsible—not others—for your actions, this is the first important step to practicing this philosophy while in college.

One strategy for maintaining this belief is to not play the blame game; for example, if you received a low grade, be honest with yourself and ask what role you played in earning the grade. Admitting you are the one responsible for your actions and then responding (and learning) from that outcome will help strengthen your self-esteem and confidence.

TAKING RISKS

Has anyone ever said, "Nothing ventured, nothing gained" to you? To take a risk can be an unsettling challenge—you can't be sure it will be worth it, you may question whether you have the ability and the desire to attempt something, and you might think about the consequences of that risk if you are unsuccessful.

Now, that's the negative approach. What if you turned this around and, instead, took a chance on something daunting? What if you decided that no matter what obstacles got in your way or what doubts crept into your mind, you would continue to pursue whatever you set out to accomplish? Imagine how you will feel when the results turn out to be positive ones.

Another way of thinking about this is "If you remain in your comfort zone you will not go any further." While taking a risk can seem difficult at first, it almost always pays off in the end—especially in the classroom.

Taking Risks in the Classroom

Your instructors have probably urged you to question rather than to simply accept everything you read or hear. If you follow this advice, you'll take risks in the classroom all the time—intellectual risks, otherwise known as critical thinking. You do this when you speak up in class, when you write an essay, and whenever you carefully rethink long-held beliefs.

Speaking Up in Class

The reward for intellectual risk-taking is that you come away with a better understanding of yourself and the world around you. But what if you are terrified of speaking up in class and of saying something dumb? What if you simply don't know where to start? Below are two case studies to help you start thinking about how to better approach intellectual risks.

Student A read the class material twice and completed all the assignments. She came to class prepared to take notes and was ready and willing to listen to what the instructor had to say on the topic being presented. As an adult student, she was used to participating in meetings at work, and she didn't feel nervous about speaking up, so she didn't think that she needed to prepare any additional material.

Student B also completed the assigned homework and believed he knew the material but also knew he would be reluctant to share his thoughts or respond to questions posed to the class. As a strategy, he wrote down several questions and responses to what he assumed would be a part of the class discussion. When he attended class, he referred to his questions and answers when those areas of discussion came up.

What were some strategies that each student employed that would help them take intellectual risks? Who do you think came to class better prepared? For each case study, what would you recommend the student do differently next time?

Exercise: Questions and Answers

What do you do to prepare for class discussions? Both Student A and Student B are good students. They read the material and did their assignments. Student B, however, uses higher-level thinking questions to help stimulate critical thinking. As you prepare for class, try to use the following generic question stems to ask questions about the material covered. Then take a few minutes to jot down your answers.

What would happen if _____?

What is the difference between _____ and _____?

What are the implications of _____?

Why is _____ important?

What is another way to look at _____?

EXAMINING EMOTIONS

Daniel Goleman, author and creator of the theory of emotional intelligence (EQ), stresses the vital role EQ plays in building self-confidence. One of his key components is emotional self-management, or the ability to make sensible decisions even when your emotions tell you to do otherwise. For example, if you received a failing grade on a quiz, your first impulse might be to get angry. Even worse, you might consider dropping the class. A better strategy would be to take the time to examine why you earned the grade that you did and to allow yourself the time needed to learn how to succeed in the course. Examining your feelings and how you react to certain situations can keep you from giving up too early on something that is challenging.

Exercise: What Makes a Success?

Make a list of the qualities you see in people you think of as confident. Share the list with someone else in your class and discuss which of these qualities have to do with feelings and interactions with other people. How many of these qualities do you see in yourself?

BEING PERSISTENT

One of the simplest ways to gain confidence is to be persistent. *Persistence* simply means the ability to stick with something through completion, even if you don't always want to. If a task or challenge seems difficult at times and the outcome may be uncertain, persistence helps you keep at it. Let's look at an example:

Imagine that you are frustrated with the teaching style of one of your instructors. She presents the material in a way that doesn't work for you (but it seems to do so for your classmates). You can elect to drop the class early in the semester and perhaps have a different teacher next time, or you could take steps that will allow you to persist in the course, such as working with a tutor, forming a study group, or meeting with your professor for clarification. In the end, you will not have given up, and your outcome could likely be a favorable one.

Ultimately, it is *your* responsibility to take charge of your success and persist—even if you have some setbacks at first. When you feel like you may be about to give up, remind yourself of your long-term goals and how persisting at the current task will help you attain those goals.

ASSERTIVENESS CHECK-UP

Answer the following questions as honestly as you can:

✔ Do you express your point of view even when it is not the same as others?

✔ Will you actually say "no" to a request made by friends or coworkers that you feel is unreasonable?

✔ How easily do you accept constructive criticism?

✔ Are you willing to ask for help?

✔ Do you make decisions or judgments with confidence?

✔ How open are you to another person's suggestions or advice?

✔ When you state your thoughts or feelings, do you do so in a direct and sincere manner?

✔ Are you likely to cooperate with others to achieve a worthwhile goal?

BEING ASSERTIVE

One of the best ways to build confidence is to let people know what you want and don't want, how you feel, and when you need help. The more skilled you are at letting people know these things, the more assertive you'll become. The more you *successfully* assert yourself, the more confident you'll become. So how do you become more assertive? Let's start by assessing where you are right now.

If you answered "yes" to less than half of the questions in the "Assertiveness Check-Up" box, the strategies below can help you feel more confident when you are attempting to be assertive.

- Use suitable facial expressions.
- Always maintain good eye contact.
- Watch your tone of voice. Your voice should be firm, audible, and pleasant.
- Be aware of your body language—how you stand, sit, and gesture.
- Actively listen to others so that you can accurately confirm what they have said.
- Ask reasoned questions when something is unclear to you.
- Take a win-win approach to solving problems: How can what you're asking for benefit both you and the person you're asking?

DEVELOPING A NETWORK

When you create a supportive network of individuals, you are being interdependent, and this is a key to fostering self-confidence. By building mutually helpful relationships, you are more likely to achieve your goals and dreams. Here are some strategies for developing this interdependence:

- Actively seek out your school's many resources. This will mean connecting with an academic advisor, signing up for a tutor if you need one, or getting involved with several on- or off-campus activities.
- Foster a valuable relationship with your instructors; ask for their assistance, feedback, and constructive criticism.
- Start a study group by looking for several classmates who are prepared, regularly attend classes, and take an active part in class discussions. Don't overlook a quiet student who may have true insight into the course; he or she can prove an asset. Approach those you've identified and suggest forming the group. If the answer is yes, decide on your group's mutual goals and the rules your group will follow.
- Coming to college can be a challenging and emotionally stressful experience; fortunately, your school offers counselors who can provide the understanding and skill to help you overcome your issues, so turning to one can be the right thing to do.

ADVICE FROM OTHER STUDENTS

The Goal Setter: Liberal Arts Major at the Community College of Rhode Island

Having little idea what he wanted to do upon entering college, the Goal Setter elected to not declare a specific major; instead he chose general education courses to slowly get himself "into the student mind-set." High school had been a struggle academically and personally, so a four-year school was not an immediate option. Previously, his only goal was to not leave school early, and now he realized he needed more structure. He connected with an advisor, and she suggested that he first take a self-assessment test and, based on the results, come up with a set of both short-term and long-term goals. The advisor explained the value in doing such an exercise and cautioned that he not give up before achieving some or all of those goals. The Goal Setter heeded this advice, earned his associate's degree, and has since transferred to a four-year college, full of confidence that his next goal of a bachelor's diploma will be realized.

The Networker: Marketing Major at Bryant University, Rhode Island

Her high school counselor told the Networker that she was "not college material," and she retained that belief until her early thirties, when she decided that she had something to prove to the counselor *and to herself*. She employed interdependence, surrounding herself with students who practiced successful strategies and who regularly encouraged her. The result was a mostly successful first-semester experience. Following this positive outcome, she never looked back, except to wait for the day when she returned to her former high school to display her diploma to her former guidance counselor.

TIPS FOR CONFIDENCE-BUILDING

Here are some time-tested strategies that will help you throughout your life. By following these steps, you will achieve *realistic and worthwhile* confidence:

- As often as possible, focus on your strong points rather than areas of weakness. In other words, be aware of what is good about you rather than what you are not proud of.
- Make a consistent effort to learn from your experiences — the good and bad (you will undoubtedly have many of both in your life).

- Find the courage to try something new and different, even when it appears too difficult or risky.
- When something bothers or disappoints you, take the time to examine your thoughts. Choose to react calmly and rationally rather than on impulse and your emotions.
- Expect that while some of what you achieve in life may be due to pure luck, a good deal more will likely be the result of your personal persistence and effort.
- Strive to be assertive. This means express how you feel, what you think, the beliefs you hold, and do so directly and sincerely. You have a right to say "no" to requests that are not genuine or reasonable.
- Continue to learn and vary your skills and talents long after you leave college. Embrace the idea that there is no end to learning throughout your life.
- Most important of all, believe in yourself. Identify what distinguishes you from everyone else and what you have to offer. Once you know these qualities, you will begin to cultivate them by applying them in everyday life.

2

MANAGING YOUR TIME

You might be the kind of student who thinks it's normal to spend hours making flash cards and outlining your notes in different colored ink. Or maybe you're an adrenaline junkie, accustomed to starting a twenty-page term paper the night before it's due.

The problem is both of these approaches carry certain inherent liabilities. Goof off and you'll probably bomb all your courses. Do nothing but cower in a library carrel for weeks on end and you'll wind up dull, pasty, and miserable. If you're like most of us, you'll learn more, get better grades, and have more fun in college if you operate somewhere in the middle.

By now, you've probably heard the Latin expression *carpe diem*, which translates to "seize the day" (as in, make time work for you). Mastering the art of time management is one key to your future success and happiness, but learning to actually make time work for you can be problematic. What can you do to take control of your own time? Read on to find out.

THE CASE FOR TIME MANAGEMENT

Why bother? We know. Some students don't want to "waste" time on planning and managing their schedules. Instead, they prefer to go with the flow. Unfortunately, the demands of college (not to mention most careers) require serious, intentional strategies. Unless you can afford to hire a personal assistant, your previous slacker habits won't carry you through.

To psych yourself up, think of time management as part of your life skill set. If you're trying to remember all the things you need to get done, it's hard to focus on actually doing the work. Organizing your time well accomplishes three things: First, it optimizes your chances for good results, so you're not flying by the seat of your pants. Second, it enhances your life by saving you from stress and regret. And finally, it reflects what you value — it's all about doing your best.

Need more motivation? Remember that people who learn good time-management techniques in college generally soar in their careers. Think about it: If you're more efficient at your job, you'll be able to accomplish more. That will give you a competitive advantage over your coworkers. Your bosses will learn to depend on you. They'll reward you with interesting projects, promotions, and educational and training opportunities. You'll feel empowered and will fill your workplace with positive vibes. You'll have time for a sizzling social life outside the office. Plus you'll make more money and need less Red Bull.

TAKING CHARGE OF YOUR TIME

Freedom can be a dangerous thing. One of the biggest differences between high school and college is that you find yourself with far more independence — and greater responsibility — than you've ever known. If you are continuing your education after a break, you may also be contending with spouse/boss/child obligations, too. But it would be a gigantic mistake to assume that Oprah, rocket scientists, and other type-A folks have some kind of monopoly on organization and focus. You, the ordinary student, can also embrace your inner executive assistant — the one who keeps you on time, on task, and ready for a slice of the action. So how do you begin?

Setting Goals

Goals help you figure out where to devote the majority of your time. To achieve your goals, you need to do more than just think about them. You need to act! This requires setting some short-term and long-term goals. When determining your long-term goals, it is important to be honest and realistic with yourself. Goals should be challenging, but they should also be attainable. Be sure they align with your abilities, values, and interests. Do you want to go on to further schooling? Have you decided what career you want to pursue? Mulling over these questions can help you start thinking about where you want to be in the next five to ten years. Dreaming up long-term goals can be exciting and fun; however, reaching your goals requires undertaking a number of steps in the short term.

Try to be very specific when determining your short-term goals. For example, if you're committed to becoming an expert in a certain field, you'll want to throw yourself into every class and internship that can help you on your way. A specific goal would be to review your school's course catalog, identify the courses you want to take, and determine when you must take them. An even more specific goal would be to research interesting internship opportunities in your field of study. The good news about goals is that each small step adds up.

Identify one long-term goal and identify three steps you can take to achieve your goal.

Long-Term Goal _____

Steps toward Your Goal

1. _____
2. _____
3. _____

Knowing Your Priorities

To achieve your goals, prioritize your life so that you're steadily working toward them.

- **Start out with a winner's mentality.** Make sure your studies take precedence. Having worked so hard to get to college, you cannot allow other activities to derail your schoolwork. Review your current commitments and prepare to sacrifice a few — for now. Whatever you do, talk to your family, your boss, and your friends about your college workload and goals so that everyone's on the same page. When you have a looming deadline, be firm. Emphasize that no amount of badgering will succeed in getting you to go to the James Bond theme party during finals week.

- **Next, start preparing for your future.** Visit your campus career center and schedule an assessment test to hone in on your talents and interests. Or, if you know what career you want to pursue, talk with a professional in that field, your guidance counselor, a professor, or an upper-class student in your chosen major to find out what steps you need to take to get the results you want, starting now. What skills and experiences should be on your résumé when you graduate that will make you stand out from the pack? Make a plan, prioritize your goals, and then make a time-management schedule.

- **Balance is key.** If you're realistic, planning for the future you want may demand big sacrifices. Be realistic about the present, too. Always include time in your schedule for people who are important to you and time on your own to recharge.

Embrace the Two-for-One Rule. For every hour you spend in class at college, you should plan to study two hours more outside of class. That's the standard, so keep it in mind when you're planning your schedule. The bottom line is that you simply carry more responsibility for your education in college than you did in high school.

TIP

Share your Google or Outlook calendar. Keeping an electronic copy of your calendar allows you to share with others at a click of the button. Letting your family, friends, and employer know what is on your plate at any given moment can bridge any misunderstandings that may arise because of your school commitments and may create a more supportive home and work environment.

Own Your Class Schedule. Your schedule will impact almost every aspect of your college life. Before you register, think about how to make your schedule work for you.

- **Start with your biorhythms.** Do you study more effectively in the day or the evening or a combination of both? Ideally, you should devote your peak hours—when you're most alert and engaged—to schoolwork. Schedule other activities, like laundry, email, exercise, and socializing, for times when it's harder to concentrate.
- **If you live on campus,** you might want to create a schedule that situates you near a dining hall at mealtimes or lets you spend breaks between classes at the library. Feel free to slot breaks for relaxation and catching up with friends. But beware the midday nap: You risk feeling lethargic afterward or even worse, oversleeping and missing the rest of your classes. If you attend a large college or university, be sure to allow adequate time to get from one class to another.

- **Try to alternate classes with free periods.** Also, seek out instructors who will let you attend lectures at alternate times in case you're absent. If they offer flexibility with due dates for assignments, all the better.
- **If you're a commuter student or carry a heavy workload,** you might be tempted to schedule your classes in blocks without breaks. But before you do this, consider the following:
  - Falling behind in all your classes if you get sick
  - The fatigue factor
  - No last-minute study periods before tests
  - The possibility of having several exams on the same day

CONTROL FACTOR: KNOW WHAT YOU *CAN* AND *CAN'T* CONTROL

When it comes to planning your time between what you can and can't control, it helps to know the difference.

WHAT YOU *CAN* CONTROL

✔ **Making good choices.** How often do you say, "I don't have time"? Probably a lot. But truth be told, you have a choice when it comes to most of the major commitments in your life. You also control many of the small decisions that keep you focused on your goals: when you wake up, how much sleep you get, what you eat, how much time you spend studying, and whether you get exercise. So be a woman or man with a plan. If you want something enough, you'll make time for it.

✔ **Doing your part to succeed.** Translation: Go to all your classes; arrive on time; buy all the required textbooks; keep track of your activities; complete every reading and writing assignment on time; take notes in class; and, whenever possible, participate and ask questions.

✔ **Managing your stress levels.** Organization is the key to tranquility and positive thinking. Manage your time well, and you won't be tormented with thoughts of all the things that need doing. Psychologists have found that free-floating anxiety can turn even your subconscious thoughts into a horror show. Want to avoid unnecessary stress? Plan ahead.

WHAT YOU *CAN'T* CONTROL

✔ **Knowing how much you'll need to study right off the bat.** Depending on the kind of high school you went to (and the types of courses you took there) or if it has been a while since you've had to study, you might be more or less prepared than your college classmates. If your studying or writing skills lag behind, expect to put in a little extra time until you're up to speed.

✔ **Running into scheduling conflicts.** If you find it hard to get the classes you need, you can seek help from a dean, an academic adviser, or someone in the college counseling center.

✔ **Needing a job to help pay your way.** Just follow the experts' rule of thumb: If you're taking a full course load, do your best to avoid working more than fifteen hours a week. Any more than that and your academic work could suffer.

FOUR TIME-WASTING HABITS TO AVOID

1. Procrastinating

Should you have to do assignments that seem incredibly long and boring? Shouldn't you be able to study with family members in the room, even if you can't get any work done with them around? Can't you occasionally blow off the outside reading? Yes, no, and no.

There are lots of reasons why we procrastinate. Maybe you're a perfectionist—in which case, avoiding a task might be easier than having to live up to your own very high expectations (or those of your parents or instructors). Maybe you object to the sheer dullness of an assignment or you think you can learn the material just as well without doing the work. Maybe you even fear success and know just how to subvert it.

None of these qualify as valid reasons to put off your work. They're just lame excuses that will get you in trouble. Fortunately, doing tasks you don't like is excellent practice for real life.

Slacker alert: Procrastination is a slippery slope. Research shows that procrastinators are more likely to develop unhealthy habits like higher alcohol consumption, smoking, insomnia, poor diet, and lack of exercise. Make sure you get these tendencies under control early. Otherwise, you could feel overwhelmed in other aspects of your life, too.

EASY TRICKS TO STOP PROCRASTINATION

✔ **Break big jobs down into smaller chunks.** Spend only a few minutes planning your strategy and then act on it.

✔ **Reward yourself** for finishing the task, like watching your favorite YouTuber or playing a game with your kids or friends.

✔ **Find a quiet, comfortable place to work** that doesn't allow for distractions and interruptions. Don't listen to music, and turn off your phone. If you study in your room, shut the door.

✔ **Treat your study time like a serious commitment.** That means no phone calls, email, text messages, or updates to your Facebook page. You can rejoin society later.

✔ **Consider the consequences if you don't get down to work.** You don't want to let bad habits derail your ability to achieve good results *and* have a life.

2. Overextending Yourself

Feeling overextended is a huge source of stress for college students. Why? Well, what constitutes a realistic workload varies significantly from one person to another. Being involved in campus life is fun and important; it's crucial not to let your academic work take a backseat.

- **Learn to say no—even if it means letting other people down.** Don't be tempted to compromise your priorities.

- **But don't give up all nonacademic pursuits.** On the contrary, students who work or participate in extracurricular activities often achieve higher grades than their less-active counterparts partly because of the important role that time management plays in their lives.

- **If you're truly overloaded with commitments and can't see a way out . . .** You may need to drop a course before the drop deadline. It may seem drastic, but a low grade on your permanent record is even worse. Become familiar with your school's add/drop policy to avoid penalties. If you receive financial aid, keep in mind that in most cases you must be registered for a minimum number of credit hours to be considered a full-time student and maintain your current level of aid. Be sure before you drop!

3. Losing Your Focus

Too many first-year college students lose sight of their goals. Translation: They spend their first term blowing off classes and assignments, then either get expelled, placed on probation, or have to spend years clawing their way back to a decent GPA. So plan your strategy and keep yourself motivated for the long haul.

4. Running Late

Punctuality is a virtue. Rolling in late to class or review sessions shows a lack of respect for both your instructors and your classmates. Arrive early and avoid using your phone in class, texting, doing homework for another class, falling asleep, talking, whispering, or leaving class to feed a parking meter. Part of managing your time is freeing yourself to focus on the present and on other people who inhabit the present with you. Note: Respecting others is a habit that can work wonders in your career and personal life.

TWO INDISPENSABLE TOOLS TO KEEP YOU ON TRACK

Here's the deal. Once you enter college or the working world, you must immediately do the following: Write down everything you need to do, prioritize your tasks, and leave yourself constant reminders. The good news is that a little up-front planning will make your life infinitely easier and more relaxing. For one thing, you'll be less likely to screw up. On top of that, you'll free your brain from having to remember all the things you need to get done so you can focus on actually doing the work. Two key items will help you plan to succeed.

TIP

Social Media Addict? Online tools like *StayFocused* allow you to block or limit your time on certain websites while you are studying so you can focus on the task at hand. Google "10 Online Tools for Better Attention & Focus" to find a program that works for you.

A Planner or Calendar

Find out if your college sells a special planner in the campus bookstore with important dates and deadlines already marked. Or, if you prefer to use an online calendar or the one that comes on your computer or smartphone, that's fine, too. As you schedule your time, follow a few basic guidelines.

Pick a time frame that works best for you. If you want a "big picture" sense of how your schedule plays out, try setting up a calendar for the whole term or for the month. For a more detailed breakdown of what you need to accomplish in the near future, a calendar for the week or even the day may be a better fit. Of course, there's no need to limit yourself—use more than one type of calendar if that works for you.

Enter all of your commitments. Once you've selected your preferred time frame, it's time to record your commitments and other important deadlines. These might include your classes, assignment due dates, work hours, family commitments, and so on. Be specific. For instance, "Read Chapter 8 in history" is preferable to "Study history," which is better than simply "Study." To be even more specific, include meeting times and locations, social events, and study time for each class you're taking. Take advantage of your smartphone and set reminders and alarms to help keep you on top of all your activities and obligations.

Break large assignments like term papers into smaller bits, such as choosing a topic, doing research, creating an outline, learning necessary computer skills, writing a first draft, and so on. And give them deadlines. Estimate how much time each assignment will take you. Then get a jump on it. A good time manager often finishes projects before the actual due dates to allow for emergencies.

Watch out for your toughest weeks during the term. If you find that paper deadlines and test dates fall during the same week or even the same day, you can alleviate some of the stress by finding time to finish some assignments early to free up study and writing time. If there's a major conflict, talk it over with your professor and find a way to work around it. Professors will be more likely to help you if you come to them plenty of time in advance.

Update your planner/calendar regularly. Enter all due dates as soon as you know them. Be obsessive about this.

Check your planner/calendar every day (at the same time of day if that helps you remember). You'll want to review the current week and the next week, too.

When in doubt, turn to a type-A classmate for advice. A hyper-organized friend can be your biggest ally when it comes to making a game plan.

A To-Do List

The easiest way to remember all the things you need to do is to jot them down in a running to-do list—updating as needed. You can do this on paper or use an online calendar or smartphone to record the day's obligations. Techies love the GTD® ("Getting Things Done"®) system for taking control of tasks and commitments. Google it to learn how it works.

1. **Prioritize.** Rank items on your list in order of importance. Alternately, circle or highlight urgent tasks. Exclamation points and stars—it's all good.
2. **Every time you complete a task, cross it off the list.** (This can be extremely satisfying.)
3. **Move undone items to the top of your next list.** (Less satisfying, but smart and efficient.)
4. **Start a new to-do list every day or once a week.** It shouldn't be just about academics. Slot in errands you need to run, appointments, emails you need to send, and anything else you need to do that day or week.

ADVICE FROM OTHER STUDENTS

Martha Flot

Education Major in Florida

"I learned a long time ago that if I don't start my work early, it's not going to happen. I always open my books right after the kids are off to school and begin with the easiest assignments. I feel really productive and get into the swing of things before tackling the harder stuff. It's kind of like the warm-up before practice."

- **Digitally bolster your memory.** "I keep everything in my smartphone calendar—for me, that's the best way to stay organized. I set reminders for all of my study groups and upcoming assignments. If it's a big exam, I'll set the reminder a week in advance to give myself plenty of time to prepare."
- **Exercise.** "I always try to exercise before I sit down for an exam or a long study session, too. Studies show that exercise boosts your blood circulation, so you can think better and feel more awake. For me, it makes a huge difference."
- **Beware of overcommitting.** "I used to be a huge people pleaser. Trying to please everyone and juggling my role as a mother, wife, and student, I learned fast that I couldn't do that and still get all my work done. Once I started prioritizing, my friends and family have been responsive and

supportive. It helps having a husband who manages his time well; you grow and learn from it."

EASY WAYS TO MAXIMIZE YOUR TIME

- ✔ **Carry work with you.** If you have a lull between classes, use it to review material from the previous class and prepare for the next one. Take advantage of waiting time (on the bus or between appointments) to study. You'll be more likely to remember what you've learned in class if you review or copy your notes as soon as you reasonably can.
- ✔ **Discipline yourself with routines.** You might want to get up early to prepare, or set fixed study hours after dinner or on weekend afternoons.
- ✔ **Don't multitask.** Even though you might be quite good at it, or think you are, the reality is—and research shows—that you'll be able to do your most effective studying and retain the most information if you concentrate on one task at a time.
- ✔ **Study with friends.** You can help each other grasp tricky concepts and memorize important facts and dates.
- ✔ **Be flexible.** Disruptions to your plans don't come with ample warning time. Build extra time into your schedule so that unanticipated interruptions don't prevent you from meeting your goals.

John Dietz

Architecture Major in Florida

"My first two years of college forced me to be a morning person. But as an upperclassman, I have the freedom to pick classes that start in the afternoon, so I've reverted to being nocturnal: I usually study or work in my design studio until 2 or 3 a.m."

- **Go digital.** "I take my computer to all my classes, so I keep a detailed calendar there. My work schedule changes frequently, so I always type that in along with all my assignments."
- **Beware of perfectionism.** "As an architect, you could spend your whole life designing something. Often I really have to tell myself to stop and go on to the next thing."
- **Find a part-time job that offers flexible hours and lets you study.** "I work at the gym on campus, where each shift is just three hours long. They only hire students, so they're very accommodating if I need to change my schedule. Plus, mostly I get to sit at the check-in desk and review my notes."

Carolina Buckler
Business and Political Science Major in Indiana

"Having a double major means a heavier workload, but it's doable in my subjects. My roommate—who's studying engineering and puts in a lot more hours than I do—couldn't have handled a heavier workload because of his major."

- **Start things sooner rather than later.** "That especially helps with group projects because it's hard to find time in everyone's schedule to get together. If you meet early, you can divide up the work."

- **Make sure your employer knows your academic commitments.** "I work twelve to fifteen hours a week as a teacher's assistant in the political science department. The professors will automatically understand if I need to take a study day. Around finals, they give everyone a week off."

- **Socialize at mealtimes.** "My friends and I meet for dinner at 5 p.m. It sounds ridiculously early, but I've found that it makes me less likely to waste time: Instead of trying to start something for an hour or so before dinner, I get back around 6:30 and jump right into homework."

3

WRITING ETHICALLY AND RESPONSIBLY

Thanks to technology, it's easier than ever for students to cheat — so cheaters are sprouting like mushrooms. Thanks to technology, it's also much easier for colleges to catch cheaters. And administrators are cracking down on cheating by making the penalties increasingly harsh.

To complicate matters, there are plenty of students who cheat *without even knowing that they're cheating.* Of course, in a perfect world, they'd get lighter sentences than the people who cheated intentionally. But colleges aren't perfect worlds. They're wonderful institutions of learning that don't like to be taken advantage of.

So let's clear a few things up.

DEFINING "CHEATING"

Cheating comes down to two things: Faking your own work and helping other students fake theirs.

Some of the Most Obvious Forms of Cheating

- Buying an essay from someone else
- Texting answers during an exam
- Sharing the details of a test with students who haven't taken it yet

- Copying someone else's homework
- Peeking at someone else's test paper
- Letting other people cheat off you
- Stealing a test
- Writing answers to the test in crazy small letters on your gum wrappers or on the inside of your bottled water label. (Note: Professors are onto these tricks.)
- Plagiarizing: The most common (but equally problematic) form of cheating

The trouble with plagiarism is that a lot of students don't completely understand what it is. Plagiarism is a fancy word that, according to the *Oxford English Dictionary*, means "taking someone else's work or ideas and passing them off as one's own." Fun fact: The word *plagiarism* comes from the Latin word for *kidnapping*. Get the picture?

It's hard to believe that anybody *really* thinks it's okay to cut and paste whole sentences from the internet into their essays. But given that some people don't think twice about downloading copyrighted music tracks and videos, maybe the concept of "borrowing" isn't as clear as it used to be. What's your stance? Have you ever lifted passages off a website, maybe even changing a couple of words to make it sound more like you? Are you inclined to believe that once something is on the web, it's public domain? If so, please know it's *not* so. The fact remains that copying or paraphrasing anything off the internet (or from any other source) and using it without citing the source is cheating.

Beware: Plagiarizing with intent is one thing. But many college students who plagiarize by accident — they copy quotations into their notes but forget to add quotation marks and later can't tell what's their own writing and what they borrowed from a source — are also convicted of plagiarism simply because they forgot to indicate which parts of an essay are their own and which parts belong to another author. We repeat: Colleges are on a crusade to thwart cheating. If your high school was lax about footnotes or paraphrasing, you need to figure out the rules fast.

THE CHEATING PROBLEM

In a recent survey of 36,000 high school students by the Josephson Institute of Ethics, 60 percent admitted to cheating on a test during the previous year. Thirty-five percent had cheated on multiple tests. A third of them had committed plagiarism, cutting and pasting from the internet. What's worse, according to recent studies by Donald L. McCabe at Rutgers University, the number of students who think that copying material from the web is "serious cheating" has plummeted to only 29 percent.

Cheating typically begins during junior high, which is—no surprise—around the same time that grade pressure and academic workloads ramp up. In college, the pressure to get good grades becomes even more intense. Maybe you're trying to get into a competitive graduate program, win a scholarship, or land a high-paying job. Maybe you're involved in a zillion clubs, sports, or volunteer activities. Maybe you have a job and/or kids. Maybe you're taking metaphysics. Whatever it is, you could start to feel overextended. And from there, you might start to justify cheating in your mind. Big mistake.

WHY YOU SHOULDN'T CHEAT

Because it's wrong. Because it's lazy and contemptible. Because getting caught could set off a firestorm and totally screw up your future. Because cheating is bad for your self-image and can trigger severe guilt and anxiety.

Because attending college is ultimately about learning new things, challenging yourself, and building your integrity. If you try to scam your way through, you've defeated the whole point of this exercise.

And here's the real drag: Cheating has a nasty way of seeping into other parts of your life, like your career, your finances, and your personal relationships, where it can cause long-term damage. Once you've cheated on a few tests, it might not seem like a big leap for you to start padding your résumé or fudging your taxes.

WHY IT'S EASY TO GET CAUGHT

College professors have more time and leeway to investigate their suspicions and better resources to back them up. Programs like Turnitin.com let instructors scan essays and crosscheck them against books, newspapers, journals, and student papers, as well as against material that's publicly accessible on the web. Even a tiny, nine-word snippet could give you away.

HOW *NOT* TO CHEAT: TEN ESSENTIAL TIPS

1. **Avoid friends who pressure you to bend the rules.** Writing a paper is really hard. Doing advanced math and science homework is really hard. Studying for exams is lonely, boring, and *really* hard. But trying to beat the system doesn't pay. Remind yourself of the consequences of cheating. Explain to your friends that you are on a valiant quest for honest

effort. Make them watch a lot of movies about Abraham Lincoln. As a last resort, find new friends.

2. **Join a study group.** If you're struggling to get through a daunting course, get together with other students to compare notes and help each other grasp tricky concepts. A study group gives you a support system and a more positive belief in yourself. It teaches you persistence and discipline because the group structure involves meeting promptly at set times for reviews. A study group can also make learning easier and more fun. Other members of the group may have noticed important points from class that you didn't catch. Plus, once you understand the material well, any impulse to cheat will cease to be an issue.

THE PENALTIES FOR CHEATING

Cheating is a much bigger deal in college than it was in high school. Remember, you're not a minor anymore. Once you're over 18 and are caught cheating, you'll be reprimanded as an adult.

✔ "At minimum, you're looking at an F for the entire course and very likely academic probation or even dismissal," says Dr. Thomas Skouras, a professor at the Community College of Rhode Island. "In most cases now, instructors have to adhere to the school's policy on cheating, so they can't bend the rules even if they want to."

✔ And it gets scarier than that: If caught cheating, you could end up with a Conviction of Plagiarism on your college transcript. That's the same transcript you'll need to use for graduate school and job applications.

✔ Plagiarism is different from other student offenses in that it isn't protected under federal confidentiality laws. Think about it: "A student who has stalked someone on campus and has a history of psychiatric illness might not have that information on his transcript," Dr. Skouras adds. "A conviction of cheating is much harder to suppress."

Note: How often are convictions of plagiarism overturned? Almost never. Most instructors won't go forward with the charges unless they have substantial evidence to back them up.

---

3. **Don't procrastinate.** Here's the deal: If you want to write a thorough and honest essay, you need to start early. College papers aren't like movie reviews. You're required to do lots of outside research. Then you have to weed through it all to figure out what's valuable. Next, you have to incorporate the highlights into an outline, a first draft, and ultimately, an original, dazzlingly brilliant work that's all your own. All of that takes time. If you leave things too late, you'll be more tempted to cheat.

> **TIP**
>
> **Make a pledge to successfully pass the course as a team—the honest way.** "I chose to form a group more than a decade ago with three other doctoral candidates, and we followed through on our promise to graduate together," says Dr. Skouras. "It really mattered that we were each rooting for the others to succeed."

4. **Don't muddle your notes.** It's vital that you keep your own writing separate from the material you've gathered from other sources. Why? Because it's surprisingly easy to mistake someone else's words for your own, especially after you get two hours into writing and your brain turns numb. So document everything. Be obsessive about this.

5. **Be a stickler for in-text citations.** It happens all the time: At the end of an essay, a student provides a full listing of all the works he or she has cited. But in the paper itself, there are no references to be found. "In this case, you're looking at a low C at best," says Dr. Skouras. "Your instructor has no choice but to take off major points since it's impossible to tell the difference between your writing and your references."

> **TIP**
>
> **Respect deadlines.** When you were in high school, your teachers might have negotiated due dates. In college, it's almost impossible to get an extension on an assignment. Your old stalling tactics ("My printer broke/I have the flu/I've been working with NASA on a nuclear laser shield—so can I get that essay to you on Monday?") won't fly.

6. **Familiarize yourself with the proper formatting for a research paper.** The MLA style is pretty much standard. If your instructors require a different style, they will let you know. If you need to learn the basic guidelines and rules for citations, The OWL at Purdue University is a great source—well written and user-friendly (**https://owl.purdue.edu**). You might also want to speak to a reference librarian. A reference librarian has a graduate degree in gathering research and can be one of your biggest allies in college. Alternately, pay a visit to the writing center on campus or talk to your instructor for advice. Many college libraries offer tutorials in MLA formatting. Getting one early in the semester can give you a big leg up.

> **TIP**
>
> **Flaunt your knowledge.** You must not only list the references you've used to research your topic, but you must also demonstrate that you know where they belong in your narrative.

7. **Be sure to list all of your research sources.** If you're not sure how to list a citation or if you're not sure that your source is valid, don't just put it down and keep your fingers crossed. Talk to your instructor or ask a reference librarian for help.

8. **Master the art of paraphrasing.** Paraphrasing means restating someone else's ideas or observations in your own words and sentences. You don't have to put the text in quotation marks, but a citation acknowledging the original source is still needed. (See *The Rules of Paraphrasing* below for examples.)

9. **If you need help, seek it early.** This sounds painfully obvious, but it's important to go to the writing center or the librarian *well before your paper is actually due*. Revision takes time and, chances are, your paper will need more than a few tweaks.

10. **If you hand something in and then realize that you used material without giving credit to the source, alert your instructor immediately.** Don't just hope it will slip through. Better to risk half a grade on one essay than your whole college career, right?

THE RULES OF PARAPHRASING

Paraphrasing doesn't mean copying a quote and swapping out a few words. It doesn't mean changing two or three words in a sequence, either. It means rephrasing someone else's quote altogether while retaining its essential meaning. Consider these examples:

> **TIP**
>
> **When copying research material into your notes, write the name of its source and page number directly after it.** Likewise, when you copy something from the internet, add a URL in brackets at the end. Use quotation marks around all cited materials. You might also try highlighting your research in a bright color to set it apart from your notes. All of this will make things easier when it's time to make your footnotes.

- If the quote is "The likelihood of an increase in the growth rate appears dim," you might change it to "The economy improving in the near future is improbable, according to Dr. X, an economist at the University of Y."
- Likewise, "Google has been working to build cars that can drive themselves," could be rewritten as "One of Google's latest projects: a robotic car that takes humans out of the driver's seat."

If you're having trouble paraphrasing something, try this trick: Put away your source material, call up a friend or your mom, and explain the point you're trying to summarize. Chances are you'll come away with something that's clear, concise, and in your own words.

A word of warning: When you paraphrase someone else's opinions or insights, you still have to document the source. The upside? You don't have to frame the passage in quotation marks.

PART TWO

WRITING ACTIVITIES

4	Patterns of Organization	35
5	Illustration	43
6	Narration	59
7	Description	78
8	Process Analysis	97
9	Definition	114
10	Division and Classification	132
11	Comparison and Contrast	150
12	Cause and Effect	167
13	Argument	185

4

PATTERNS OF ORGANIZATION

PREWRITING ACTIVITIES

Trying out patterns of organization as single paragraphs or extended multi-paragraph examples is a good way to find a pattern that works well, given your topic, audience, and purpose.

Illustration: Paragraphs or Essays

Illustration paragraphs or essays use examples to explain unfamiliar concepts. Try completing the following prompts to get ideas for an example paragraph or essay.

- All of my favorite _____ have one trait in common: _____.

- I often have to explain _____, and the examples I use are _____ _____.

- _____, _____, and _____ are all good examples of _____ _____.

Now write a sentence of your own that could jump-start an example:

_____

_____

_____

Narration: Paragraphs or Essays

Narration tells a story about an event or a sequence of events in order to explain something. Try completing the following prompts to get ideas for a narrative paragraph or essay.

- I would never have been able to do _____ if it weren't for the time when _____.

- At the time, I had no idea how the events of the day when _____
  _____ [something happened] _____
  would affect me.

- The most exciting experience of my life was _____
  _____
  because _____.

Now write a sentence of your own that could jump-start a narrative:

_____

_____

_____

Description: Paragraphs or Essays

Descriptive writing uses sensory details to contribute to a dominant impression. Try completing the following prompts to get ideas for a descriptive paragraph or essay.

- The taste of _____ always reminds me of _____.

- _____ never smells better than it does when _____.

- _____'s voice makes me feel _____.

Now write a sentence of your own that could jump-start a description:

_____
_____
_____

Process Analysis: Paragraphs or Essays

Process analysis explains, step by step, how something works or how to do something. Try completing the following prompts to get ideas for a process analysis paragraph or essay.

- I have insider knowledge of the way _____ works, and it's not what most people think.

- You might be surprised at how easy it is to _____ _____.

- When I _____, I _____ _____ first, then _____, and finally _____.

Now write a sentence of your own that could jump-start a process analysis:

_____
_____
_____

Definition: Paragraphs or Essays

A definition or extended definition conducts a close analysis of a complicated idea or word. Try completing the following prompts to get ideas for a definition paragraph or an extended definition essay.

- Many people are not aware that _____ means _____ and not _____.

- When I first heard of _____, I thought it meant _____.

Now write a sentence of your own that could jump-start a definition paragraph or essay:

_____

_____

_____

Division and Classification: Paragraphs or Essays

Division and classification writing looks closely at the parts that make up a whole or different categories or types of something. Try completing the following prompts to get ideas for a division and classification paragraph or essay.

- Based on my experience as a(n) _____, _____ can be divided into the following types: _____ _____.

- All of the _____ I've ever seen can be categorized as _____, _____, _____, or _____.

- On this campus, the food options can be classified as follows: _____ _____ _____.

Now write a sentence of your own that could jump-start a division and classification paragraph or essay:

_____

_____

_____

Comparison and Contrast: Paragraphs or Essays

Comparison and contrast analyzes the similarities and differences between two people, places, policies, activities, ideas, or other things. Try completing the following prompts to get ideas for a comparison-and-contrast paragraph or essay.

- _____ and _____ may seem very different, but they have more in common than you might think.

- I thought I would like _____ more than _____, but it turned out otherwise.

- The toughest decision I ever had to make involved choosing between _____ and _____, both of which were _____.

Now write a sentence of your own that could jump-start a comparison-and-contrast analysis:

_____
_____
_____

Cause and Effect: Paragraphs or Essays

Cause-and-effect paragraphs and essays show how one or more causes lead to or influence something else. Try completing the following prompts to get ideas for a cause-and-effect paragraph or essay.

- I'm glad that _____ happened; because of it, _____.
- The unexpected consequences of _____ included _____ and _____.
- When _____ happened, we had to know why. After a long search, we learned _____.

Now write a sentence of your own that could jump-start a cause-and-effect paragraph or essay:

_____
_____
_____

Argument: Paragraphs or Essays

An argument aims to convince or persuade readers to believe something or take some action. Try completing the following prompts to get ideas for an argument paragraph or essay.

- Because _____ causes problems such as _____ and _____, we should take action to _____.

- Every _____ should have the opportunity to _____, and that dream can come true if _____.
- Even more than _____, children need _____, and _____ can help.

Now write a sentence of your own that could jump-start an argument paragraph or essay:

_____
_____
_____

ESSAY ORGANIZATION ACTIVITIES

Identifying Possible Topics for an Essay That Mixes Patterns of Organization

Reread the ideas you've generated and choose one or more that contain an idea you might want to use in an essay that mixes patterns of organization. Look particularly closely at any ideas you find yourself addressing more than once in the prompts you have completed.

- A possible preliminary topic is _____
_____.

- Another possible preliminary topic is _____
_____.

- A third possible preliminary topic is _____
_____.

Identifying the Readers I Want to Reach in an Essay That Mixes Patterns of Organization

Figuring out what your audience already knows and does not know about the topic you choose will be extremely important. If you consider what they already believe or know, you will be able to identify methods that will work more effectively to reach them. Complete the following prompts to analyze the audience you expect to reach:

- My audience includes _____.
- They may already know _____ about this topic, but they may not know _____ _____.
- I need to tell this audience about _____ _____ so they will understand my perspective on the topic.
- When they read my essay, I want them to feel _____ _____.
- My purpose for writing is to _____.

Brainstorming Ideas for an Essay That Mixes Patterns of Organization

Which of the patterns will be most useful to you in drafting an essay on one of your preliminary topics? Choose at least two or three patterns and spend five minutes brainstorming all the ideas you can think of for a paragraph or section using that pattern.

Pattern	**Pattern**	**Pattern**
_____	_____	_____
Ideas for use	**Ideas for use**	**Ideas for use**
_____	_____	_____
_____	_____	_____
_____	_____	_____
_____	_____	_____
_____	_____	_____
_____	_____	_____

Moving from Topic to Preliminary Thesis for an Essay That Mixes Patterns of Organization

Fill in the blanks to start thinking about the point you want to make in your essay.

- Many people will be surprised to find out that _____
  _____.

- I used to believe _____, but now I think
  _____.

- This may sound strange, but [the topic] makes me think about _____
  _____ because _____.

- At first I did not understand [the topic], but now I think of it as _____
  _____.

- A new insight my readers should have about [the topic] is _____
  _____.

Now, write your own generalization that can serve as a preliminary thesis:
_____
_____
_____

Creating a Graphic Organizer or Outline to Plan Your Essay Mixing Patterns of Organization

You may use whatever organizational method makes sense for the patterns you choose and the topic and audience you aim to reach. An effective way to begin is to create a graphic organizer or outline that notes which pattern you will use to make a given point.

Drafting, Reviewing, Revising, and Editing Your Essay Mixing Patterns of Organization

Pay attention to the pattern that seems to govern your overall essay. When you are sure which main pattern you want to use, go to the chapter in this Student's Companion detailing that pattern and complete the activities there for drafting, getting feedback, revising, and editing your work.

5

ILLUSTRATION

PREWRITING ACTIVITIES

Finding Ideas for an Illustration Essay Topic

An illustration essay uses multiple examples to support a generalization or clarify an unfamiliar concept. To identify a generalization or concept that can serve as the topic for your illustration essay, try the following prompts.

- Most people don't understand _____, but I do.
- A big problem that many people aren't aware of is _____ _____.
- The common thread that connects all my favorite films is _____ _____.
- The biggest problems facing my community have _____ _____ in common.

Try it yourself!

Identify a general truth or a concept that you can illustrate with examples.

_____
_____
_____

Clustering to Brainstorm Ideas for an Illustration Essay Topic

To generate ideas for the topic of an illustration essay, try clustering. Write an idea, either for an example or for a concept you will illustrate with examples, in the middle of a sheet of paper and circle it. Then, write more words and phrases that relate to the central word, circling each and joining them to the central circle. Keep going, generating ideas related to circled concepts as you think of them, until the paper is filled. (You can also use software for digital clustering diagrams if you prefer.)

- What ideas were most productive for you, prompting the largest clusters of circled words and phrases?
- Are any ideas unexpectedly unproductive, going nowhere on your diagram? Pay attention to what doesn't work as well as to what does.

Identifying a Preliminary Topic for an Illustration Essay

What general statement or concept will you illustrate using examples in your essay? The topic can be one that you started with on pages 43–44, or it can be an idea that came to you while you were exploring something else in one of the activities above.

- My preliminary topic is _____
_____
_____.

Finding a Perspective on the Preliminary Topic for Your Illustration Essay

In order to find examples that will work well for your illustration essay, you should consider your point of view of the topic.

- This topic makes me feel _____
_____.

- I want anyone who reads my example essay to know that _____
_____.

- The best way to show my point of view is to include _____,
  _____, and _____.

Identifying the Readers I Want to Reach in My Illustration Essay

Figuring out what your audience already knows and does not know about the topic will be extremely important. If you consider what they already believe or know, you will be able to identify examples that can more effectively illustrate the concept you are explaining. Complete the following prompts to analyze the audience you expect to reach.

- My audience includes _____.
- They may already know _____
  about this topic, but they may not know _____
  _____.
- I need to tell this audience about _____
  _____ so they
  will understand my perspective on the topic.
- When they read my essay, I want them to feel _____
  _____.
- My purpose for writing is to _____.
- To succeed in this purpose, I will probably need to use _____ (one or two/three or four/five or more) _____ examples.

Exploring Example Ideas for an Illustration Essay

What examples should you use to illustrate the generalization or concept of your topic? Respond to any of the following prompts that are appropriate for your example essay.

- The field or discipline that will provide the most compelling examples for my audience is _____
  because _____.
- An example that everyone associates with this topic is _____
  _____.
  It is (useful/not useful) for my example essay because _____
  _____
  _____.

- A visual that would clarify the topic is _____.
- My own experience with _____
  could be used as an example because _____
  _____.
- Other examples might include _____,
  _____,
  and _____.
- I (need/do not need) to use sources from research.
- Additional sources I could use include _____
  _____, and
  I can find them _____.

Identifying Strong, Vivid Examples for an Illustration Essay

Detailed examples make an illustration essay come alive. Brainstorm as many of the following prompts as possible to try out different patterns of organization for the examples you will include, and be sure to include vivid details to interest readers.

- narrative examples

    EXAMPLE: a personal anecdote to illustrate the concept of decluttering

- descriptive examples

    EXAMPLE: a detailed description of a local grocery store's cereal aisle to illustrate the concept of choice overload

- process analysis examples

    EXAMPLES: a description of the process of writing an essay to illustrate the idea of multitasking

- causal analysis examples

    EXAMPLES: a discussion of the effect of a neighborhood cleanup to illustrate the "broken windows" theory

    _____
    _____
    _____

- Try creating an example from any method of development that seems useful.

    _____
    _____
    _____

Choosing Visuals or Other Media to Enliven an Illustration Essay

If you have access to photos or other media that will help create a vivid impression of the generalization you are illustrating, consider including one or more of them in your essay. Video and audio files can be used in an essay that you will post online.

THESIS ACTIVITIES

- My preliminary topic (p. 44) is _____.

Narrowing and Focusing a Topic for an Illustration Essay

Will you be able to clarify the concept or support the generalization in an essay of the assigned length? Sometimes a narrower topic may allow you to create a better example essay.

- If I had five minutes to explain the concept or generalization to people who are not familiar with it, I would start with _____
    _____.

Identifying a Point for Your Illustration Essay

To me, the single most important thing about the topic I am trying to illustrate is (pick one and complete the sentence)

- that it clarifies _____.
- that it helps people understand _____.

- that it proves _____.
- that it is exciting because _____.
- that it is important because _____.
- that _____
  _____.

Moving from Topic to Preliminary Thesis for an Illustration Essay

Fill in the blanks to start thinking about the point you want to make in your example essay.

1. Many people will be surprised to find out that _____
   _____.

2. I used to believe _____, but now
   I think _____.

3. This may sound strange, but (the topic) makes me think about
   _____ because _____.

4. At first I did not understand (the topic), but now I think of it as _____
   _____.

5. A new insight my readers should have about (the topic) is _____
   _____.

   Now, write your own generalization that can serve as a preliminary thesis.
   _____
   _____
   _____

Testing Your Thesis

In a sentence or two, explain your proposed thesis for your illustration essay to a classmate or friend who is part of your audience, and briefly tell him or her about the example or examples you will use to support the thesis. Ask for responses to these questions.

- How much do you understand about the generalization being illustrated?
  _____
  _____

- How does the plan for this illustration essay seem likely to expand your understanding of the generalization, idea, or concept?
  _____

- What interests you most about this topic? Why? _____
_____

Do the reviewer's responses suggest that you are on the right track? If not, consider whether you should rethink your topic, review your assumptions about what your audience knows and cares about, or reconsider the examples you will use.

DRAFTING ACTIVITIES
Deciding Where to Begin

Begin at the easiest point for you to get started. If starting with the example that is most personal or most familiar will help you get your draft underway, begin there. If you know you want to include an image or video clip as an example, begin with that. You can start with the introduction, of course, but you do not have to begin at the beginning; you can draft the introduction and conclusion after completing the body of your essay if you like.

Brainstorming Ways to Get Readers' Attention

Keeping your preliminary thesis in mind, try your hand at these effective ways to start an introduction.

- a quotation (something you said, something someone said to you, a relevant snippet of dialog that will be part of one of your examples)
_____
_____

- an anecdote or story (something that sheds light on the subject you are describing or explains how you came to realize the importance of your topic)
_____
_____

- a provocative statement (a surprising or shocking announcement or an unexpected revelation)
_____
_____

- a question that prompts readers to think about how they will answer it
_____
_____

- a hypothetical situation that invites others to imagine being in someone else's place

  _____
  _____

- a comparison that shows how your unfamiliar concept is like something more familiar to your readers

  _____
  _____

Drafting an Introduction

Choose the opening you like most from the examples you've created, and start a new draft that begins with that opening. How can you move from this catchy opening to your first example?

- Where will you state your thesis — right after the opening, at the end of the introduction, or somewhere else?
- What background information will readers need right up front to make sense of your examples? How can you incorporate it smoothly?
- How will you help readers get a sense of the scope of the examples you will use to illustrate your thesis?

Trying Options for Organizing Body Paragraphs

If you aren't certain what organization makes sense for the examples that will support your thesis, try completing the most viable option listed below. Use the option you choose as the basis for an outline or graphic organizer that you can follow as you draft.

By Time

- Chronological order: start at the beginning and move forward in time
- Reverse chronological order: move from most recent time to earliest

In Order of Importance, Familiarity, or Interest

- Least to most important, familiar, or interesting: save the best for last
- Most to least important, familiar, or interesting: start strong

Try it yourself!

- Organization plan for examples: _____

Drafting Activities

Topic of first body paragraph: _____

- I will develop the example(s) using the _____ method.

    Details to include in the paragraph:

    - _____
    - _____
    - _____

Topic of second body paragraph: _____

- I will develop the example(s) using the _____ method.

    Details to include in the paragraph:

    - _____
    - _____
    - _____

Topic of third body paragraph: _____

- I will develop the example(s) using the _____ method.

    Details to include in the paragraph:

    - _____
    - _____
    - _____

(Continue until you have outlined or sketched a plan for all your body paragraphs.)

Drafting a Conclusion

Your conclusion should reinforce the way your examples have illustrated your generalization and make a final statement.

- These examples illustrate _____.
- This example is important because _____.
- Readers should feel _____.

Try it yourself!
Draft a conclusion that reinforces your thesis and ties the whole essay together.

_____
_____
_____

Creating an Intriguing Title

Your title should indicate the topic of your illustration essay and say something about it that will interest readers. Try the following ideas to create an intriguing title that your audience will want to read:

- Alliteration: My generalization relates to _____ and some words that begin with the same sound and relate to my examples are _____.

- Groups of three: Three things that are important to the example are _____, _____, _____, and _____.

- Question: People ask _____ _____ about this generalization.

- Quotation: Someone said "_____ _____" about the topic I am writing about.

- Try out a title of your own: _____

FEEDBACK ACTIVITIES

Getting Your Questions Answered by Peer Reviewers

You'll get better feedback from peer reviewers if you ask for specific help with comments and questions like these.

- I'm not sure whether or not _____ is working.
- Does the example about _____ make sense?
- My biggest concern is _____.

Now write the question with which you *most* want your peer reviewers' help.

_____

_____

Asking Reviewers for Feedback about an Illustration Essay

To find out if reviewers are getting the impressions you want to give in your illustration essay, have them answer the following questions.

- What is the thesis? Is it interesting?
- How clearly do the examples illustrate the thesis? Which example(s) do you like best? Which do you like least?
- What questions are not answered that should be answered?
- What details work well in the examples? What do you like about them?
- Which details are weakest? Which ideas need further development?
- Does the essay's organization make sense?
- How well does the essay hang together? How effective are the transitions between paragraphs?
- How enticing is the introduction? Which parts make you want to keep reading? What is less interesting?
- How well does the conclusion end the essay? What works best to bring the essay to an end? What should change?
- How effective is the title? Why?
- My favorite part of this essay is _____

    _____

    because _____.

- The part that I think needs the most improvement is _____

    _____

    because _____.

Conducting a Self-Review

Put your draft aside for at least one day. Then, read it again, doing your best to pretend that you have never seen it before. Use the Rubric for Assessing Illustration Essays to see how well you think you have accomplished the essay's objectives in this draft. (Your instructor may use other criteria for assessing student writing, so be sure to check with him or her about expectations.)

Rubric for Assessing Illustration Essays

	Exceeds expectations	Meets expectations	Needs improvement	Does not meet expectations
Focus, purpose, and audience	The thesis addresses a term or concept that is interesting and important to the audience. The introduction indicates how the essay will clarify, explain, or support the thesis by using examples, and promises an insight or learning experience. Unified body paragraphs have clearly focused topic sentences.	The thesis addresses a claim, term, or concept appropriate to the audience and the assignment. The introduction clearly indicates the intent to clarify or support the thesis by using examples. Unified body paragraphs include functional topic sentences.	A thesis is evident but is too broad or narrow, or does not meet the assignment's purpose or appeal to the target audience. Body paragraphs are too broadly or too narrowly focused, or lack clearly governing topic sentences. Some irrelevant material may be included.	No clear thesis is evident, or the thesis is inadequate to control the essay or engage the reader's favorable attention. Body paragraphs lack topic sentences, or are too long or too short to effectively develop individual subtopics.
Development	The essay offers well-chosen, authoritative, representative, relevant, and concrete examples to clarify and support the paper's thesis and engage the audience's favorable attention. The writer's extended examples are fully integrated with the paper's explanatory content; personal experience examples are balanced with historical, topical, or other examples that can be authenticated.	Examples are appropriate to the audience and purpose, and sufficient to adequately support the thesis, but may be left to "speak for themselves" without being fully integrated with the paper or paragraph topic. Essay and paragraph content is relevant, with no disruption of essay or paragraph unity and no visible bias.	Examples are offered to support the thesis, but are too broad or too general to fully engage the audience or validate the thesis. Development may be overbalanced with unverifiable personal experience or hypothetical examples.	Few examples are offered, or they distort or confuse the thesis rather than serving to validate or clarify it.

	Exceeds expectations	Meets expectations	Needs improvement	Does not meet expectations
Organization and coherence	Clear, logical organizing principles govern the arrangement of content at both essay and paragraph levels. Forecasting statements are used effectively in the introduction. Smooth, largely unnoticed transitions within and between ideas and paragraphs enhance coherence.	Development is reasonably organized throughout. Sentences within paragraphs are arranged to show the logical sequencing of ideas. Each body paragraph is unified and coherent. Body paragraphs are sequenced effectively for the type(s) of examples that writer employs. Transitions link ideas and paragraphs.	Organization is attempted but is ineffective or unclear. The reader can follow the writer's points only with difficulty. Body paragraph sequencing seems uncontrolled or random, with insufficient or confusing transitional, organizational cues being employed.	The essay has no discernible organization at essay or paragraph level. The reader is unable to follow the writer's train of thought, and the essay employs inadequate or misleading transitional devices or organizational cues.
Style and structure	Introductory, body, and concluding elements engage the audience's attention and guide it through the essay's coherent body paragraphs. A conclusion prompts rethinking of the topic or promotes new insight. The essay achieves variety in sentence pattern and type. If using sources, the writer uses signal phrasing and clearly sets off cited from original material. Tone is skillfully controlled; word choice is apt.	The introduction is relevant and sets the tone, and guides the reader into the body of the paper that is developed in multiple paragraphs. A functional conclusion is present. Sentences are well constructed if not varied. If used, sources are acknowledged, but signal phrasing or parenthetical elements may be misplaced or confusing. Diction is appropriate, but may be repetitive or imprecise.	Paragraphing is weak. Introductory elements are not controlled, and a separate body and conclusion may not be included. Sentences are vague or ambiguous, with little or no variety in pattern or type. If outside sources are used, no in-text citation is offered, or it is too confusing to clearly distinguish the writer's work from cited material. Tone is inappropriate for the purpose and audience. Diction is faulty or inappropriate.	Paragraphing is absent or insufficient to meet the demands of the writing situation, with no distinct introductory or concluding elements included. Sentences are difficult to interpret; the writer does not demonstrate control of grammar or paragraph structure. Tone and diction are confusing, contradictory, or inappropriate.

	Exceeds expectations	Meets expectations	Needs improvement	Does not meet expectations
Precision and editing	All elements of grammar, usage, and mechanics are mastered. Listed examples are punctuated properly and are parallel. Outside sources, if used, are cited in proper bibliographic form. Formatting conventions are applied appropriately throughout. An attractive page design draws the reader's eye through the page. The writer executes the assignment memorably with no careless errors.	The essay is largely free of errors in grammar, punctuation, and mechanics. Sentences are coherent, and structural errors (where present) do not disrupt the reading. Outside sources, if used, are cited, with minor lapses in form or format. The paper is neat, legible, and clear, with formatting consistently applied. The paper satisfies the assignment with only scattered careless errors.	The essay has frequent errors in grammar, punctuation, and mechanics. Outside sources, when used, are cited, but formatted incorrectly, sometimes leading to ambiguity of source or source type. Errors in manuscript formatting conventions draw unfavorable attention. The writer attempts but fails to fully execute the assignment. Numerous careless errors distract, though perhaps cause little or no confusion.	Verb and pronoun usage, sentence construction, and diction are consistently faulty. Punctuation is arbitrary. Where outside sources are used, bibliographic entries are omitted or incomplete. Careless or illegible writing is confusing. Stains, tears, blots, or printing errors distract the reader and may make parts of the paper unreadable. The writer fails to observe manuscript conventions or to satisfy other demands of the assignment. Errors throughout are serious enough to cause confusion and obscure meaning.

Gathering Responses and Collecting Your Thoughts

Gather all the reviewer responses. Make notes about what you and your reviewers agree and disagree on, moving from most important issues, such as appropriateness of the topic, the effectiveness of the examples, the organization, and the support for ideas, to least important, such as spelling and comma placement. List areas where you agree that improvement is needed, and make a plan about what you need to revise. Think about areas of disagreement, too. You make the final decisions about what changes to make, so determine which comments you need to respond to and which you can ignore.

REVISION AND EDITING ACTIVITIES
Identifying Options for Revision Planning

After you have gathered revision comments on your early draft from peer reviewers and your instructor (pp. 52–53), choose one of the following strategies to begin making your revision plan.

- Create a storyboard. On a sticky note or note card, write the generalization you are illustrating and put it at the top of your work area. Using separate sticky notes or note cards for each paragraph or example, write down important features such as topic sentences and supporting details. Does your organization make sense? Do the parts work together? Does every paragraph help to advance the story and clarify the point it makes? Using sticky notes or note cards of a different color, add notes to each paragraph about how you will strengthen, change, or delete content based on your reviewers' comments and your own. Take photos of the parts of the storyboard so you'll have a record of what you decide, even if you lose your notes.

- Create a graphic organizer. Using either paper and pencil or a digital document, create text boxes representing each introductory paragraph, body paragraph, and conclusion paragraph, and write the main idea of each paragraph in the box. Below it, leave room to revise the main idea. To the right of each main idea box, draw additional boxes for changes, additions, and deletions you have decided to make to supporting details, transitions, and other material in that paragraph.

- Make an annotated outline. Using formal complete sentences or informal phrases, make an outline that shows the current main ideas, supporting details, and organization of your draft. Using highlighters, colored pens, different colors of type, or some other method to make your changes clearly visible, annotate your outline to show the changes you plan to make to your thesis, dominant impression, organization, supporting ideas, introduction, conclusion, and so on.

- Make a plan of your own. _____
_____
_____
_____

Revising an Illustration Essay

Following the plan you've created, write a complete revised draft. Repeat as needed until you feel that you have a solid draft that is nearly final.

Using Your Common Issues to Focus Editing of Your Illustration Essay

Edit for grammar, punctuation, and other common problems you have.

- The two kinds of problems that teachers or peer reviewers point out most often in my writing are _____ and _____.
- I know I sometimes struggle with _____.

Review the information in Part 3 (pp. 205–42) about the errors you have identified above. Then reread your draft again, correcting any such errors and other issues that you find.

Proofreading

- Run the spellchecker and carefully consider every suggestion. Do not automatically accept the suggestions! Remember that spellcheckers cannot identify problems with certain kinds of words, such as homonyms and proper nouns (names), so check the spelling of such words yourself. Write the words you have misspelled on a spelling checklist you can use to identify and avoid words that give you trouble.
- Read your essay aloud slowly, noting and correcting any issues that you find.
- Read your essay aloud backward, word by word, looking for repeated words and similar mistakes that are easy to miss in work that is very familiar. Correct any problems you see.

When your work is as error-free and professional as you can make it, submit your essay.

6

NARRATION

PREWRITING ACTIVITIES

Finding Ideas for a Narrative Essay Topic

What story can you include in your narrative? Try these prompts while you're starting to think about a topic:

- The ___[superlative adjective — funniest/scariest]___ thing that I ever experienced happened when ___[person]___ did ___[action]___ because ___[reason]___.

- When my ___[relation to me — mother/granddad/pet snake]___ did ___[action]___, I realized ___[surprising thing]___.

- ___[experience]___ was almost a[n] ___[really good or bad thing]___.

- ___[person]___ didn't want to do ___[action]___ but did it anyway because ___[reason]___.

- ___[person]___ discovered that she/he was [different from/not different from] others in the ___[place or community]___ when ___[event]___ happened.

Help a classmate! Write a "mad lib" with blanks and ask others to complete it:

_____
_____
_____

Collaborating to Brainstorm Ideas for a Narrative Essay Topic

If you're having trouble thinking of ideas, try brainstorming with a group of classmates. Spend five minutes writing as many sentences as you can in response to one or more of the following prompts:

- The moment when everything changed for me was _____
  _____.

- The moment when everything changed for my family was _____
  _____.

- The moment when everything changed for _____
  was _____.

After five minutes, each member of the group should choose one or two of the sentences and briefly share the narrative(s). As each person tells a story, the other group members should ask questions, and the storyteller can make notes about details, sequence of events, and other important ideas that the story needs to include. Determine which of the narrative options that each person presents would make the most compelling essay.

Identifying a Conflict in Your Narrative

What conflict or important choice faced you (or the person your narrative is about)? Try responding to any of these prompts that are relevant, or create a statement of your own that identifies the conflict in your story.

- [I/The person I'm writing about] would never have _____
  if [I/the person] hadn't been afraid of _____
  _____.

- When [I/the person I'm writing about] heard _____,
  _____ [I/the person]
  knew that it was important to _____.

- [I/The person who is featured in the narrative] had to choose between
  _____, which mattered

because _____, and
_____, which mattered because
_____.

Exploring Topic Ideas for a Narrative Essay

What details should you include in your narrative? Choose the previous prompt that has produced the story you most want to tell, and try at least two of the following ideas to start collecting details for use in your narrative essay.

- Look at photos or videos that relate in some way to the event you will narrate. What do you see? Who is in the photos and videos? Where were the images taken? What else about your narrative do they remind you of?

- Take five minutes and make a list of all the words and phrases that come to mind when you think about the experience you will narrate. Circle the ones that seem most important. How can you use them as you tell the story?

- Talk to people who remember the experience you want to narrate. What do they recall about it? How are their memories like and unlike yours?

- Take a photo of an object, person, or place related to your experience. Print the image in the middle of a blank piece of paper. Use the space around the image to describe its significance in your narrative and to make notes about how to include the photo in your essay.

- Write down dialog from an incident you will include in your narrative essay, or re-create the dialog in a recording. Who said the words and why? What was the mood and tone of the dialog?

Identifying a Preliminary Topic for a Narrative Essay

What will your narrative be about? The topic can be one that you started with on page 59, or it can be an idea that came to you while you were exploring something else in one of the previous activities.

- My preliminary topic is _____
_____
_____.

Identifying Sensory Details for a Narrative Essay

How can you make your story immediate and interesting for readers? Details make a narrative come alive. Brainstorm as many of the following prompts as possible, identifying sensory details that reinforce your point of view on the topic and the setting you will describe.

- something seen, observed, watched that is important to the story

    EXAMPLES: the mirage that appeared to be a pool of water on the steaming blacktop, the uneven layers of the collapsing wedding cake

- dialog or other sound heard or overheard that contributes to the story

    EXAMPLES: "Why can't I come in?" my little brother whined; the whistle of a freight train in the middle of the night as it passed behind our house going far away

- an aroma, smell, or stench that figures importantly in the story

    EXAMPLES: the scent of lilacs reminding me of final exam time, the rotting vegetable smell from the bottom of the garbage bag as we rummaged for our lost lottery ticket

- something tangible or textured that contributes to the story

    EXAMPLES: the sharp blade that I wasn't supposed to touch, the grimy fur of the stray kitten

- a flavor or taste that matters to the story

    EXAMPLES: the deliciously charred taste of the marshmallows that had fallen into the campfire, sweet and juicy little tomatoes from my uncle's backyard

Thinking about the Setting for a Narration

A narrative essay should set a scene.

- The story I am telling happened when [I/the person I am writing about] was _____ years old, in _____ [year or era].

- The story is most strongly tied to _____ [place].

- Whenever I think of [this story], I remember being _____ _____ and doing _____.

- When I remember this time and place, I always think of _____, _____, and _____.

Thinking about Action for a Narration

A good narrative includes some kind of action. Try at least one of the following activities to enliven the action in your narrative.

- Draw a picture of the action in your narrative. Who is in the picture? What is happening?

- Identify a verb to describe every action in your story. Then try finding at least three more precise synonyms for each verb, using a thesaurus if necessary. Which verbs are liveliest?

- Record yourself three separate times telling the active event of your narrative. Play your narratives back for a friend. Which version is best? Why?

Finding a Perspective on the Preliminary Topic for Your Narrative Essay

- Thinking about this topic makes me feel _____ _____.

- Others involved in the event I will narrate felt _____ _____.

- I want anyone who reads my narrative essay to know that _____ _____.

- The best way to show my point of view is to include _____ _____, and _____.

Identifying the Readers I Want to Reach in My Narrative Essay

- My audience includes _____.
- Their experiences have probably been [similar to/different from] the one I am describing.
- I need to tell this audience about _____
  _____ so they will understand my perspective on the topic.
- When they read my essay, I want them to feel _____
  _____.
- My purpose for writing is to _____.

THESIS ACTIVITIES

- My preliminary topic (p. 61) is _____.

Narrowing and Focusing a Topic for a Narrative Essay

Can you tell the story in your narrative briefly, and will it support some kind of point you're making? Will you be able to tell the story and make the point in an essay of the assigned length? Sometimes a narrower topic allows you to create a better narrative essay.

- If I had five minutes to explain why this story is important, I would start with
  _____
  _____.

Identifying a Point for Your Narrative Essay

To me, the single most important thing about this narrative is (pick one and complete the sentence)

- that it made me realize _____.
- that it made someone else realize _____.
- that it started _____.
- that it ended _____.
- that it changed _____.

- that _____.

Moving from Topic to Preliminary Thesis for a Narrative Essay

Fill in the blanks to start thinking about the point you want to make about your narrative.

1. Many people will be surprised to find out that _____.

2. I used to believe _____, but now I think _____.

3. This may sound strange, but [the story] makes me think about _____ because _____.

4. I did not expect what happened to make much of an impression on me, but _____.

5. The reason my readers should care about [the story] is _____.

Now, invent your own assertion about your topic that can serve as a preliminary thesis.

Testing Your Thesis

Tell the story you will include in your narrative essay to a classmate, friend, or peer group. Ask this person to respond to these questions.

- What is the takeaway from this narrative? _____

- The point of the story is to _____.

Do their responses match the point you were trying to make? If not, consider whether you should change the narrative or reconsider the point the story is making.

DRAFTING ACTIVITIES

Planning the Placement of Your Thesis

In a narrative essay, a thesis stating the point of your narrative will usually appear at the beginning of the story or at its end, or it can be unstated, just implied.

- Do readers need to hear the story before the thesis will make sense? If so, stating the thesis in your introduction does not make sense.
- Should I state the thesis directly, or should it be implied? Even if you decide not to state it directly, be sure that the thesis is clear to readers.

Deciding Where to Begin

For many people, the best way to begin a narrative essay is to tell the story first, since the story is probably the part of the essay you can draft most easily. However, if you have an idea for a solid jumping-off place that will help you write coherent body paragraphs, you can begin with an introduction. (You can even begin by writing the conclusion first if you feel that it will be the easiest place to get started.)

Brainstorming Ways to Get Readers' Attention

Keeping your narrative and your preliminary thesis in mind, try your hand at these effective ways to start an introduction:

- a quotation (something you said, something someone said to you, a relevant snippet of dialog from the narrative)

_____
_____

- an anecdote or story (something that sheds light on the subject you're describing or explains how you came to realize the importance of your topic)

_____
_____

- a provocative statement (a surprising or shocking comparison or an unexpected revelation)

_____
_____

- a question that prompts readers to think about how they will answer it

_____
_____

- a hypothetical situation ("Have you ever tried to . . . ?") that invites others to imagine being in someone else's place

  _____
  _____

- a comparison of the topic with something more familiar to your readers

  _____
  _____

Drafting an Introduction

Choose the opening you like most from the examples you've created, and start a new draft that begins with that opening. How easily can you move from this catchy opening to your narrative? Try one of the following activities if you are having trouble creating an introduction.

1. Write your opening sentence at the top of a page and label it "A." Then write the main point of your narrative at the bottom of the page and label it "B." Ask a classmate or friend to write three to five words or phrases that can get you from A to B.
2. Using any of the words or phrases that seem useful, write three sentences to connect your opening to the beginning of your narrative. The final sentence should wrap up the introductory paragraph and also set up the first sentence of the narrative that will follow. If you have decided to include an explicit thesis statement in your introduction, the final sentence will probably be your thesis.

Trying Options for Organizing Body Paragraphs

A narrative is usually organized by sequencing events in a clear order, and details should build tension to the climactic moment of the essay. If you aren't certain what organization makes sense for your narrative essay, try completing any option that seems viable. Use the option you choose as the basis for an outline or graphic organizer that you can follow as you draft your narrative.

By Time
Chronological order (starting at the beginning and moving forward)

- First, _____.
- Then, _____.
- Finally, _____.

Out of order (flashback or arrangement by association)
- A little while ago, _____.
- Before that, _____.
- Now, _____.

In Order of Importance, Familiarity, or Interest
Least to most important, familiar, or interesting (saving the best for last)
- Least _____.
- More _____.
- Most _____.

Most to least important, familiar, or interesting (starting strong)
- Most _____.
- Less _____.
- Least _____.

Try it yourself!
Topic of first body paragraph: _____
 Details to include in the paragraph:
- _____
- _____
- _____

Topic of second body paragraph: _____
 Details to include in the paragraph:
- _____
- _____
- _____

Topic of third body paragraph: _____
 Details to include in the paragraph:
- _____
- _____
- _____

(Continue until you have outlined or sketched a plan for all your body paragraphs.)

Drafting a Conclusion

Your conclusion should reinforce the point of your narrative without being repetitive or boring. If you have not stated the thesis explicitly in the introduction or body of your narrative essay, you should either state it explicitly or imply it in your conclusion.

- The point of this narrative is _____ _____.

- Readers should know that I feel _____ _____.

- Readers should feel _____ _____.

- A detail that suggests my thesis is _____ _____.

- A reason that I chose to tell the story here and now is that _____ _____.

Try it yourself!

Draft a conclusion that reminds readers — or explicitly tells them for the first time — what the point of your story is:

_____
_____

Creating an Intriguing Title

Your title should indicate your topic and say something about it that will interest readers. Try the following ideas to create an intriguing title that your audience will want to read:

- Alliteration: My story is about _____, and some words that begin with the same sound and relate to my point are _____.

- Groups of three: Three things that are important to the narrative are _____, _____, and _____.

- Question: People ask _____
  _____ about my story.
- Quotation: Someone said "_____
  _____" about my narrative.
- Try out a title of your own: _____

FEEDBACK ACTIVITIES

Getting Your Questions Answered by Peer Reviewers

You'll get better feedback from peer reviewers if you ask for specific help with comments and questions like these:

- I'm not sure whether or not _____ is working.
- Does the story about _____ make sense?
- My biggest concern is _____.

Now write the question with which you *most* want your peer reviewers' help:

_____

_____

Asking Reviewers for Feedback about a Narrative Essay

To find out if reviewers are getting the impressions you want to give in your narrative essay, have them answer the following questions.

- What is the thesis? Does it need to be clearer? Should it be implied rather than stated directly (or vice versa)?
- How clearly is the narrative told? How clear is the point of the story?
- What questions are not answered that should be answered?
- Is the point of the narrative clear?
- What details work well for the narrative? What do you like about them?
- Which details are weakest? Which ideas need further development?
- Does the essay's organization make sense?
- How well does the essay hang together? How effective are the transitions between paragraphs?

- How enticing is the introduction? Which parts make you want to keep reading? What is less interesting?
- How well does the conclusion end the essay? What works best to bring the essay to an end? What should change?
- How effective is the title? Why?
- My favorite part of this essay is _____

because _____.

- The part that I think needs the most improvement is _____

because _____.

Conducting a Self-Review

Put your draft aside for at least one day. Then, read it again, doing your best to pretend that you have never seen it before. Use the Rubric for Assessing Narration Essays, and rate the draft yourself. (Your instructor may use other criteria for assessing student writing, so be sure to check with him or her about expectations.)

Rubric for Assessing Narration Essays

	Exceeds expectations	Meets expectations	Needs improvement	Does not meet expectations
Focus, purpose, and audience	The narrative focuses on a specific incident from the writer's experience for the purpose of expressing a view or feeling, for informing, or persuading the target audience. The introduction briefly establishes the setting and	The thesis addresses an appropriately limited incident that is meaningful to the audience and that meets the assignment. The introduction indicates the writer's purpose — to tell a story in order to make	A thesis is apparent but the paper addresses a topic too broad to be described as an incident (such as the senior year in high school) or that fails in some other way to satisfy the assignment's requirements or appeal to the	No clear thesis or narrative point is evident, or the paper does not have a clear purpose or engage the reader's favorable attention. Impressions and vague abstract statements may generally relate to an identified

	Exceeds expectations	Meets expectations	Needs improvement	Does not meet expectations
	purpose, sets the tone, and gives the audience a reason to read. A clear thesis gives purpose to the narrative and controls all development.	a point or share an insight or life lesson — but the point may be too obvious or too personally confessional for an academic audience. The thesis focuses all or most of the development.	target audience. Body paragraphs may be analytical rather than narrative (for example, "I learned three things about myself in my senior year"). Some irrelevant content may be included.	topic but do not form a narrative sequence. Irrelevant material may intrude or contradictory material may confuse the reader about the paper's focus or purpose.
Development	The paper offers well-chosen, concrete details and images along with natural dialog to vividly re-create the incident being narrated. Unobtrusive, insightful commentary or explanation supports the thesis and engages the audience's favorable attention. Exposition and forecasting statements offer helpful context. Characters seem real.	Details and dialog serve to engage the audience and accomplish the narrative purpose and are sufficient to adequately support the thesis, but may not be fully integrated, leaving the reader to wonder at their significance. Content is relevant, with no disruption of essay or paragraph unity and no distortion or visible bias. Characters are appropriately developed.	Details and dialog are sparse, overbalanced by statements that tell about the incident rather than relating or narrating it directly. Analytical or explanatory observations may inappropriately constitute the bulk of the essay's development. Irrelevant observations or opinions may intrude and distract the reader or obscure the point. Characters are developed but may be depicted unrealistically.	Few or no details or dialog is included. General statements are vague or they distort or confuse the thesis rather than serving to validate or clarify it. No effort to re-create a scene or narrate an incident is apparent. No exposition is offered, or it is not clearly related to the incident. Characters are flat and undeveloped, so they are unengaging.

	Exceeds expectations	Meets expectations	Needs improvement	Does not meet expectations
Organization and coherence	A clear chronological sequence governs development at both essay and paragraph levels. Flashbacks and forecasting statements are used effectively throughout and are marked clearly with well-chosen transitional devices. Dialog proceeds naturally and changes in speaker are clearly marked. Explanatory discourse is woven through the narrative and relates consistently to linking elements in the introduction and conclusion, framing the incident and reinforcing the thesis.	Development is reasonably organized throughout, arranged to show the chronological sequencing of sentences narrating the incident, but may be perfunctory. Exposition and forecasting statements are signaled with adequate transition. Indirect quotation may replace dialog. Transitions are adequate but may be used repetitively. Focusing statements in the introduction and conclusion help provide context. The narrative purpose is achieved.	Chronological organization is attempted but inconsistent, so coherence is weak. The reader can discern a sequence of events but can only follow it with difficulty, as exposition and explanation are inserted with little transition. Conversations are not represented as dialog. Transitions are used improperly, randomly, or repetitively. The introduction and conclusion fail to clarify the narrative purpose or create a context.	The essay has no discernible organization at essay or paragraph level. Unconnected impressions fail to provide a cohesive narrative structure. No expository or explanatory content is introduced, and the essay employs inadequate or misleading transitional devices or organizational cues. No contextualizing statements are included in either introduction or conclusion; the narrative purpose is obscure.

	Exceeds expectations	Meets expectations	Needs improvement	Does not meet expectations
Style and structure	Design of introductory and body elements engage the audience's favorable attention and guide it through the essay's content, arranged in coherent body and dialog paragraphs. A conclusion prompts rethinking of the topic or promotes new insight. The paper achieves variety in sentence pattern and type. Tone is skillfully controlled and avoids being too stiff, informal, or familiar; word choice is apt and artful.	The introduction addresses the topic, sets the tone, and guides the reader into the body of the paper, which is developed in multiple separate paragraphs and dialog. A functional conclusion is present. The writing employs little variety, but sentence construction is competent. Tone and diction are generally appropriate to audience or purpose, but may be self-conscious, colloquial, repetitive, or imprecise.	The essay uses spacing or indention, but paragraphing is weak. Introductory and concluding elements may not be present to frame the narrative. In dialog, changes in speaker are not properly signaled by the beginning of a new paragraph. Sentences employ faulty or mixed constructions, with little or no variety in pattern or type. Tone and diction are inappropriately stiff or informal for the purpose and audience.	Paragraphing is absent or insufficient to meet the demands of the writing situation, with no distinct introductory or concluding elements included. Dialog is not represented, or the speaker of a given passage cannot be definitively identified. Sentences are difficult to interpret; the writer does not demonstrate control of grammar or paragraph structure. Tone and diction are contradictory or inappropriate.

Feedback Activities

	Exceeds expectations	Meets expectations	Needs improvement	Does not meet expectations
Precision and editing	The writer reveals mastery of all elements of grammar, usage, and mechanical conventions. Verb tenses are consistent, with appropriate shifts in passages of exposition and forecasting. Uses of second person perspective and passive voice are absent. Dialog is punctuated properly and is interspersed with exposition and explanation to provide variety to the eye when perusing the page. The writer executes the assignment memorably with no careless errors.	The essay is largely free of error in grammar, punctuation, and use of mechanical conventions, though occasional lapses occur. Verb tenses may shift, and inappropriate shifts in person may occasionally be included, but do not create confusion. Dialog is punctuated well, with only minor and infrequent errors. The paper is neat, legible, and clear, with formatting of manuscript conventions applied consistently. The paper satisfies the assignment with only scattered editing errors.	The essay is weakened with frequent errors in grammar, punctuation, and the use of mechanical conventions. Punctuation of dialog includes frequent errors; shifts in verb tense and perspective are pervasive and distracting. The submission may be crumpled, stained, or torn. Errors in manuscript formatting conventions draw unfavorable attention. Numerous editing errors distract the reader, though perhaps cause little or no confusion.	Verb and pronoun usage, sentence constructions, and diction are consistently faulty. Sentence structure is dysfunctional. Punctuation is unconventional. The reader is unable to follow attempts at dialog. Careless or illegible writing is confusing. Stains, rips, blots, or printing errors distract the reader and may make parts of the paper unreadable. The writer fails to observe manuscript conventions or to satisfy other demands of the assignment. Errors throughout are serious enough to cause confusion and misunderstanding of meaning.

Gathering Responses and Collecting Your Thoughts

Gather all the reviewer responses. Make notes about what you and your reviewers agree and disagree on, moving from most important issues, such as the interest of the narrative, the effectiveness of the story's point, the organization, and the support for ideas, to least important, such as spelling and comma placement. List areas where you agree that improvement is needed, and make a plan about what you need to revise. Think about areas of disagreement, too. You make the final decisions about what changes to make, so determine which comments you need to respond to and which you can ignore.

REVISION AND EDITING ACTIVITIES
Identifying Options for Revision Planning

After you have gathered revision comments on your early draft from peer reviewers and your instructor (pp. 70–71), choose one of the following strategies to begin making your revision plan.

- Create a storyboard. On a sticky note or note card, write the main point of your narrative and put it at the top of your work area. Using separate sticky notes or note cards for each paragraph or example, write down important features such as topic sentences and supporting details. Does your organization make sense? Do the parts work together? Does every paragraph help to advance the story and clarify the point it makes? Using sticky notes or note cards of a different color, add notes to each paragraph about how you will strengthen, change, or delete content based on your reviewers' comments and your own. Take photos of the parts of the storyboard so you'll have a record of what you decide, even if you lose your notes.

- Create a graphic organizer. Using either paper and pencil or a digital document, create text boxes representing each introductory paragraph, body paragraph, and conclusion paragraph, and write the main idea of each paragraph in the box. Below it, leave room to revise the main idea. To the right of each main idea box, draw additional boxes for changes, additions, and deletions you have decided to make to supporting details, transitions, and other material in that paragraph.

- Make an annotated outline. Using formal complete sentences or informal phrases, make an outline that shows the current main ideas, supporting details, and organization of your draft. Using highlighters, colored pens, different colors of type, or some other method that will make your changes clearly visible, annotate your outline to show the changes you plan to make to your thesis, dominant impression, organization, supporting ideas, introduction, conclusion, and so on.

- Make a plan of your own: _____
_____
_____

Revising a Narrative Essay

Following the plan you've created, write a complete revised draft. Repeat as needed until you feel that you have a solid draft that is nearly final.

Using Your Common Issues to Focus Editing of Your Narrative Essay

Edit for grammar, punctuation, and other common problems you have.

- The two kinds of problems that teachers or peer reviewers point out most often in my writing are _____ and _____.

- I know I sometimes struggle with _____.

Review the information in Part 3 (pp. 205–42) about the errors you have identified above. Then reread your draft again, correcting any such errors (and any other issues) that you find.

Proofreading

- Run the spellchecker and carefully consider every suggestion. Do not automatically accept the suggestions! Remember that spellcheckers cannot identify problems with certain kinds of words, such as homonyms and proper nouns (names), so check the spelling of such words yourself. Write the words you have misspelled on a spelling checklist you can use to identify and avoid words that give you trouble.
- Read your essay aloud slowly, noting and correcting any issues that you find.
- Read your essay aloud backward, word by word, looking for repeated words and similar mistakes that are easy to miss in work that is very familiar. Correct any problems you see.

When your work is as error-free and professional as you can make it, submit your essay.

7

DESCRIPTION

PREWRITING ACTIVITIES

Brainstorming Memories to Find a Good Descriptive Topic

Prod your memory with questions about sensory details.

- The most delicious thing I have ever eaten is _____.
- A sound that always makes me happy is _____.
- The ugliest place I have ever seen was _____.
- I experienced the worst pain of my life when _____.
- For me, the smell of _____ is always associated with _____.
- The object I cherish most is _____ because _____.
- The person who makes me feel most _____ is _____ because _____.

Try one of your own.

_____
_____
_____
_____

Freewriting to Expand Ideas for a Descriptive Essay

Choose the prompt that creates the *most vivid* ideas in your mind and spend five minutes freewriting (or record yourself speaking) without stopping, giving every detail you can think of about the sense, thing, place, person, or feeling you've identified. You can use words, phrases, or complete sentences; you can jump from one idea to another if a new thought comes to mind. Time yourself, and don't stop writing or speaking until the time is up.

Identifying a Useful Preliminary Topic for a Descriptive Essay

What person, place, animal, plant, thing, or idea seems like a good preliminary topic for a descriptive essay? The topic can be one that you started with on pages 78–79, or it can be an idea that came to you while you were freewriting about something else.

- My preliminary topic is _____
_____
_____.

Finding a Perspective on the Preliminary Topic

- Thinking about this topic makes me feel _____
_____.

- I want anyone who reads my essay to know that _____
_____.

- The best way to show my point of view is to include _____,
_____, and _____.

Identifying the Readers You Want to Reach

- My audience includes _____.
- They might be interested in this topic because _____
_____
_____.
- I need to tell this audience about _____
_____.
so they will understand how I feel about the topic.
- When they read my essay, I want them to feel _____
_____.
- My purpose for writing is to _____.

Finding Sensory Details to Support the Impression of a Descriptive Essay

Brainstorm as many of the following prompts as possible, identifying sensory details that reinforce your point of view on the topic and the setting you will describe.

- something seen, observed, or watched that connects to the setting and contributes to the dominant impression

    EXAMPLES: bright dots on a Twister mat, a sunset turning the ocean pink

    _____
    _____

- something heard or overheard that connects to the setting and contributes to the dominant impression

    EXAMPLES: the faraway motorcycle sound of a hummingbird, impatient honking behind me as my car wheezed and died

    _____
    _____

- an aroma, smell, or stench that connects to the setting and contributes to the dominant impression

    EXAMPLES: the cloyingly sweet smell of baby powder lingering in a room she had left, the scent of cut grass perfuming a summer night

    _____

    _____

- something tangible or textured that connects to the setting and contributes to the dominant impression

    EXAMPLES: sharp gravel pinching my bare feet, the mule's flannel-soft ears

    _____

    _____

- a flavor or taste that connects to the setting and contributes to the dominant impression

    EXAMPLES: my grandfather sprinkling salt on a juicy slice of watermelon, the herbal sore-throat remedy that tasted like the sole of a muddy army boot

    _____

    _____

Using Specific Words to Emphasize the Feeling Readers Should Take Away from a Descriptive Essay

Reread your supporting details and cross out any that are irrelevant or that give a different impression than the one you want readers to get. You may want to ask a classmate or peer group if the details you plan to keep are effective.

Finding Figures of Speech to Enliven a Description

Practice making comparisons to bring your topic to life.

- If this topic were a person, it would be _____ because _____.

- _____ reminds me
  of _____ because
  _____.

- People say that _____ is
  like _____, but I don't
  think that is true because _____
  _____.

  Now try writing your own comparison.

  _____
  _____
  _____

THESIS ACTIVITIES

- My preliminary topic (from p. 79) is _____
  _____.

Narrowing and Focusing a Topic for a Descriptive Essay

Is your preliminary topic something that you can describe in an essay of the assigned length? Sometimes a narrower topic allows you to create a better description.

- To me, the single most important thing about this topic is (pick one and complete the sentence)
  - that it made me realize _____.
  - that it is unique because _____.
  - that it reminds me of _____.
  - that the person's character is _____.
  - that _____
    _____.

- If I had five minutes to explain why I have strong feelings about this topic, I would start with _____
  _____.

Moving from Topic to Thesis for a Descriptive Essay

Fill in the blanks to start thinking about making some kind of assertion (that is, expressing an opinion or taking a stand) about your topic.

1. Many people are surprised to find out that (my topic) is _____
   _____.

2. I used to believe _____ about (my topic), but now I think _____
   _____.

3. This may sound strange, but (my topic) reminds me of _____ because _____.

4. I did not expect (my topic) to make much of an impression on me, but _____.

5. The reason audiences should care about (my topic) is _____
   _____.

6. An ordinary _____ is like _____, but (my topic) is different because _____
   _____.

7. Invent your own assertion about your topic.
   _____
   _____
   _____

Creating a Preliminary Thesis Statement for a Descriptive Essay

Remember that a thesis statement needs a topic—but it also needs to make some kind of assertion about the topic. In a descriptive essay, the thesis should emphasize the dominant impression you want your writing to make on readers.

- _____ has brightened my life since the day _____.
- I changed my mind about _____ after experiencing _____.

Reread the ideas you've come up with about your topic on pages 78–82, and try writing a thesis statement of your own.

_____
_____
_____
_____

Developing a Dominant Impression for a Descriptive Essay

The main idea in a descriptive essay is a dominant impression—an overall attitude, mood, or feeling that readers are left with.

- What dominant impression should your thesis evoke? Write a few words that evoke the same impression in you, and refer to them frequently as you write.

Thinking about the Setting for a Description

A descriptive essay evokes a very particular setting.

- The memory I am writing about happened when I was _____ years old, in _____ (year or era).

- The memory is most strongly tied to _____ (place).

- Whenever I think of (my topic), I remember being _____
  _____
  and doing _____.

- When I remember this time and place, I always think of _____,
  _____, and _____.

DRAFTING ACTIVITIES

Deciding Where to Begin Your Draft

What part of the draft are you most excited about writing or do you feel best prepared to begin? Start with that part. If you know how you want to tell your story but not how you want to introduce or conclude, begin with body paragraphs. If you have an idea for a solid jumping-off place that will help you write coherent body paragraphs, begin with an introduction. You don't need to write the draft in what will be its final order; just get started.

Brainstorming Ways to Get Readers' Attention

Keeping your thesis, setting, and dominant impression in mind, try your hand at these effective ways to start an introduction.

- a quotation (something you said, something someone said to you, a quotation from a book or film, etc.)

  _____

- an anecdote or story (something that sheds light on the subject you're describing or explains how you came to realize the importance of your topic)

  _____

- a provocative statement (a surprising or shocking comparison or an unexpected revelation)

  _____

- a question that prompts readers to think about how they will answer it

  _____

- a hypothetical situation that invites others to imagine being in someone else's place

  _____

- a comparison of the topic with something more familiar to readers

  _____

Drafting an Introduction

Choose the opening you like most from the examples you've created, and start a new draft that begins with that opening. Then write the preliminary thesis that you created on page 84. How easily can you move from a catchy opening sentence to your preliminary thesis?

1. Write no more than three sentences to connect your opening and your thesis.
2. Copy and paste your opening statement, connecting sentences, and preliminary thesis into a new document. Revising any of the sentences as needed, write a complete introductory paragraph.

Trying Options for Organizing Body Paragraphs

If you aren't certain what organization makes sense for your descriptive essay, try completing as many of the following options as you can. Which one best reinforces the dominant impression you want your essay to give? Use the option you choose as the basis for an outline or graphic organizer that you can follow as you draft.

By Time
Chronological order (starting at the beginning and moving forward)

- First, _____.
- Then, _____.
- Finally, _____.

Reverse chronological order (starting at the end and moving backward)

- Now, _____.
- Earlier, _____.

Out of order (flashback or arrangement by association)

- A little while ago, _____.
- Before that, _____.
- Now, _____.

By Place

- If I moved around the place I am describing while describing it, I would begin with _____
  and end with _____.

In Order of Importance, Familiarity, or Interest
Least to most important, familiar, or interesting (saving the best for last)

- Least _____.
- More _____.
- Most _____.

Most to least important, familiar, or interesting (starting strong)

- Most _____.
- Less _____.
- Least _____.

Try it yourself!
Topic of first body paragraph: _____

    Details to include in the paragraph:

- _____
- _____
- _____

Topic of second body paragraph: _____

    Details to include in the paragraph:

- _____
- _____
- _____

Topic of third body paragraph: _____

    Details to include in the paragraph:

- _____
- _____
- _____

(Continue until you have outlined or sketched a plan for all your body paragraphs.)

Drafting a Conclusion

Your conclusion should reinforce the dominant impression you are giving in your essay without being repetitive or boring.

- The dominant impression I want this description to give is _____ _____.

- Readers should know that I feel _____ _____.

- Readers should feel _____.

- A fact, story, or detail that reminds readers of my thesis is _____ _____.

- A reason that I chose to describe this topic and this setting here and now is that _____.

Try it yourself!

Draft a conclusion that reminds readers of your dominant impression without repeating your thesis exactly as you've stated it in the introduction:

_____
_____
_____
_____

Creating an Intriguing Title

Your title should indicate your topic and say something about it that will interest readers. Try the following ideas to create an intriguing title that your audience will want to read.

- Alliteration: My topic is _____, and some words that begin with the same sound and relate to my topic are _____.

- Groups of three: Three things I talk about in the essay are _____ _____, _____ _____, and _____.

- Question: People ask _____ _____ about my topic.

- Quotation: Someone said "_____ _____" about my topic.

- Try out a title of your own: _____

FEEDBACK ACTIVITIES

Getting Your Questions Answered by Peer Reviewers

You'll get better feedback from peer reviewers if you ask for specific help with comments and questions like these.

- I'm not sure whether or not _____ is working.

- Does the story about _____ make sense?

- My biggest concern is _____.

Now write the question with which you *most* want your peer reviewers' help.

_____
_____

Asking Reviewers for Feedback about a Descriptive Essay

To find out if reviewers are getting the impressions you want to give in your descriptive essay, have them answer the following questions.

- What is the thesis? What is your dominant impression?
- How well do the topic sentences of the body paragraphs support the dominant impression?
- What important questions do you have that are not answered by the essay?
- What details work best for this essay? What do you like about them?
- Which details are weakest? Which ideas need further development?
- Does the essay organization make sense?
- How well does the essay hang together? How effective are the transitions between paragraphs?
- How enticing is the introduction? Which parts make you want to keep reading? What is less interesting?
- How well does the conclusion end the essay? What works best to bring the essay to an end? What should change?
- How effective is the title? Why?
- My favorite part of this essay is _____

  because _____.

- The part that I think needs the most improvement is _____

  because _____.

Conducting a Self-Review

Put your draft aside for at least one day. Then, read it again, doing your best to pretend that you have never seen it before. Use the Rubric for Assessing Description Essays, and rate your draft yourself. (Your instructor may use other criteria for assessing student writing, so be sure to check with him or her about expectations.)

Rubric for Assessing Description Essays

	Exceeds expectations	Meets expectations	Needs improvement	Does not meet expectations
Focus, purpose, and audience	The description focuses on a specific person, place, or thing from the writer's experience to express a view or feeling, inform, or persuade the target audience. The introduction briefly establishes the focus of attention, sets an engaging tone, and gives the audience a reason to read. A clear thesis gives the essay a meaningful purpose and controls all development.	The thesis addresses an appropriately limited, specific subject of description that engages the audience and meets the assignment. The introduction indicates the writer's purpose—describing in order to share, teach, or convince—but the subject may be overly personal for an academic writing situation. The thesis statement and topic sentences effectively focus content at the essay and body levels.	A focus of description is apparent, but the thesis fails to clarify the purpose for the writing, satisfy the assignment's requirements, or appeal to the target audience. The introduction is sparse or vague. Body paragraphs may follow an analytical, explanatory, or narrative method of development rather than using description. Some irrelevant content may be included.	No clear thesis or focal point for description is evident, or the paper does not have a clear purpose or engage the reader's favorable attention. Impressions and generalizations may refer to an identified topic but do not develop or re-create a specific image, impression, moment, or place. Irrelevant material may intrude or contradictory material may confuse the reader about the paper's focus or purpose.

	Exceeds expectations	Meets expectations	Needs improvement	Does not meet expectations
Development	The paper offers specific, clear details and images evoking multiple sensory responses to depict the subject of description. Natural, insightful commentary or explanation clarifies the purpose for which the imagery is offered and engages the audience's favorable attention. Imagery is constructed of strong, concrete nouns and avoids using too many intensifiers or modifiers.	Details serve to engage the audience and accomplish the description's purpose. Imagery may be primarily visual or focus on only one of the senses. Details adequately support the thesis, but may be more ornamental than functional. Content is relevant, with no disruption of essay or paragraph unity and no distortion or visible bias. Imagery evokes feeling or understanding but avoids sentimentality or overreliance on modifiers.	Details and specifics are sparse, and development is comprised of general observations rather than concrete imagery relating directly to the subject of description. Most imagery is included for the sake of ornament. Personal observations or opinions may be less helpful or meaningful than merely distracting. Imagery is trite and figures of speech predominate rather than original imagery, making the essay either dry or overly sentimental.	Few or no details or concrete, specific images are included. General statements are vague or they obscure the thesis rather than serving to validate or clarify it. No recreation or depiction of a scene or other subject of description is discernible. If imagery is present, its purpose is not clearly related to the support of a thesis or the achievement of a purpose. Very little sensory stimulation occurs, as imagery is undeveloped, relying heavily on repetitive intensifiers and modifiers.

	Exceeds expectations	Meets expectations	Needs improvement	Does not meet expectations
Organization and coherence	A clear organizing principle (spatial, emphatic, or other) governs the arrangement of content at both essay and paragraph levels. Organizing cues are used effectively. Each body paragraph has its own internal organization, which relates to linking elements in the introduction, other body paragraphs, and conclusion. The reader understands at every point what is being described, why it is being described, and how the description relates to the essay's purpose.	Development is reasonably organized throughout, arranged according to some logical principle, but may be predictable or mechanical. Shifts in the reader's field of vision are signaled with adequate transition. Body paragraphs follow the sequence mapped in the introduction and summarized in the conclusion, but the rationale behind the sequencing itself may be unclear. Transitions are adequate but may be used repetitively. The essay's descriptive purpose is adequately achieved.	A strategy is attempted for sequencing material but is not implemented consistently, so arrangement of content seems uncontrolled. The reader can follow a sequence of impressions but only with difficulty, as exposition and explanation are inserted with little transition. Organizing cues are used improperly, randomly, or repetitively. The introduction and conclusion fail to clarify the thesis, and the body paragraphs lack coherence, so the essay's descriptive purpose is not achieved.	The essay has no discernible organization at essay or paragraph level. Random impressions fail to provide a cohesive structure at either the essay or the paragraph level. No explanatory content is introduced, and the essay employs inadequate or misleading transitional devices or organizational cues. No contextualizing statements are included in either introduction or conclusion; the paper seems comprised of general impressions largely unconnected to a descriptive purpose.

	Exceeds expectations	**Meets expectations**	**Needs improvement**	**Does not meet expectations**
Style and structure	Design of introductory and body elements engages the audience's favorable attention and guides it through the essay's content, arranged in coherent body and dialog paragraphs. A conclusion prompts rethinking of the topic or promotes new insight. The paper achieves variety in sentence pattern and type. Tone is skillfully controlled and avoids being too stiff, informal, or familiar; word choice is apt and artful.	The introduction addresses the topic, sets the tone, and guides the reader into the body of the paper, which is developed in multiple separate paragraphs. A functional conclusion is present. The writing employs some variety of pattern or type, and sentence construction is competent. Tone and diction are generally appropriate to audience or purpose, but may be too formal or informal for the rhetorical situation.	The essay uses spacing or indention, but paragraphing is weak. Introductory and concluding elements may not be present to frame the purpose for which the subject is being described. Changes in subtopics are not properly signaled by the beginning of a new paragraph. Sentences employ faulty or mixed constructions, with little or no variety in pattern or type. Tone and diction are inappropriately stiff or informal for the purpose and audience.	Paragraphing is absent or insufficient to meet the demands of the writing situation, with no distinct introductory or concluding elements included. Shifts in person or verb tense are frequent and random. Sentences are difficult to interpret; the writer does not demonstrate control of grammar or paragraph structure. Tone and diction are contradictory or inappropriate.

	Exceeds expectations	Meets expectations	Needs improvement	Does not meet expectations
Precision and editing	The writer reveals mastery of all elements of grammar, usage, and mechanical conventions. Verb tenses are consistent, with appropriate shifts in passages of exposition and forecasting. Uses of second person perspective and passive voice are absent or appropriate if included. Sequential modifiers are punctuated properly and are interspersed with exposition and explanation to provide variety. The writer executes the assignment memorably with no careless errors.	The essay is largely free of errors in grammar, punctuation, and use of mechanical conventions, though occasional lapses occur. Inappropriate shifts in verb tense and person may occasionally be included, but do not create confusion. Sequential modifiers are punctuated correctly, with only minor and infrequent error. The paper is neat, legible, and clear, with formatting of manuscript conventions applied consistently. The paper satisfies the assignment with only scattered careless errors.	The essay is weakened by frequent errors in grammar, punctuation, and the use of mechanical conventions. Punctuation of sequential modifiers includes frequent errors; shifts in verb tense and perspective are pervasive and distracting. The submission may be crumpled, stained, or torn. Errors in manuscript formatting conventions draw unfavorable attention. Numerous careless errors distract the reader, though perhaps cause little or no confusion.	Verb and pronoun usage, sentence constructions, and diction are consistently faulty. Sentence structure is dysfunctional. Punctuation is unconventional. Careless or illegible writing is confusing. Stains, rips, or printing errors distract the reader and may make parts of the paper unreadable. The writer fails to observe manuscript conventions or to satisfy other demands of the assignment. Errors throughout are serious enough to cause confusion and misunderstanding of meaning.

Gathering Responses and Collecting Your Thoughts

Gather all the reviewer responses. Make notes about what your reviewers agree and disagree on, moving from most important issues, such as thesis, dominant impression, organization, interest, and support for ideas, to least important, such as spelling and comma placement. List areas where you agree that improvement is needed, and make a plan about what you need to revise. Think about areas of disagreement, too. You make the final decisions about what changes to make, so determine which comments you need to respond to and which you can ignore.

REVISION AND EDITING ACTIVITIES

Identifying Options for Revision Planning

After you have gathered revision comments on your early draft from peer reviewers and your instructor (pp. 88–89), choose one of the following strategies to begin making your revision plan.

- Create a storyboard. On a sticky note or note card, write your thesis statement or dominant impression and put it at the top of your work area. Using separate sticky notes or note cards for each paragraph or example, write down important features such as topic sentences and supporting details. Does your organization make sense? Do the parts work together? Does every paragraph help to support the dominant impression? Using sticky notes or note cards of a different color, add notes to each paragraph about how you will strengthen, change, or delete content based on your reviewers' comments and your own. Take photos of the parts of the storyboard so you'll have a record of what you decide, even if you lose your notes.

- Create a graphic organizer. Using either paper and pencil or a digital document, create text boxes representing each introductory paragraph, body paragraph, and conclusion paragraph, and write the main idea of each paragraph in the box. Below it, leave room to revise the main idea. To the right of each main idea box, draw additional boxes for changes, additions, and deletions you have decided to make to supporting details, transitions, and other material in that paragraph.

- Make an annotated outline. Using formal complete sentences or informal phrases, make an outline that shows the current main ideas, supporting details, and organization of your draft. Using highlighters, colored pens, different colors of type, or some other method to make your changes clearly visible, annotate your outline to show the changes you plan to make to your thesis, dominant impression, organization, supporting ideas, introduction, conclusion, and so on.

- Make a plan of your own. _____
_____
_____

Revising a Descriptive Essay

Following the plan you've created, write a complete revised draft. Repeat as needed until you feel that you have a solid draft that is nearly final.

Using Your Common Issues to Focus Editing of Your Descriptive Essay

Edit for grammar, punctuation, and other common problems you have.

- The two kinds of problems that teachers or peer reviewers point out most often in my writing are _____ and _____.

- I know I sometimes struggle with _____.

Review the information in Part 3 (pp. 205–42) about the errors you have identified above. Then reread your draft again, correcting any such errors (and any other issues) that you find.

Proofreading

- Run the spellchecker and carefully consider every suggestion. Do not automatically accept the suggestions! Remember that spellcheckers cannot identify problems with certain kinds of words, such as homonyms and proper nouns (names), so check the spelling of such words yourself. If you keep track of the words you commonly misspell, you can improve your spelling, so consider a spelling-mistake list based on what you find.
- Read your essay aloud slowly, noting and correcting any issues that you find.
- Read your essay aloud backward, word by word, looking for repeated words and similar mistakes that are easy to miss in work that is very familiar. Correct any problems you see.

When your work is as error-free and professional as you can make it, submit your essay.

8

PROCESS ANALYSIS

PREWRITING ACTIVITIES

Getting Started with a Process Analysis Topic

Complete the following prompts to start thinking about topics for an essay on how to do something or how something works.

- I know better than most people how to _____.
- I learned how to _____ when I was young.
- I am interested in how _____ because _____.
- Most people think that the best way to _____ is _____, but they are mistaken.
- From observing _____, I learned how _____ works.

Now try one of your own.

_____

_____

_____

Collaborating on Ideas for a Process Analysis Essay

Working with two or three classmates, come up with a familiar task (making a sandwich, completing a homework assignment) and list the steps for the *worst possible* way to accomplish it. Include as many vivid concrete details and specific actions as you can. Share this with the class as a whole.

Freewriting to Come Up with Ideas for an Analysis of How Something Works

Spend five minutes writing without stopping about a system you are familiar with (such as a machine you understand or a process you know well at home, work, or school). When you finish, underline or highlight the most important parts of the process you have described. What needs more explanation? What can you omit? What do you need to add?

Identifying a Useful Preliminary Topic for a Process Analysis Essay

What process or system seems like a good preliminary topic for a process analysis essay? The topic can be one that you started with on p. 97, or it can be an idea that came to you while you were freewriting about something else.

- My preliminary topic is _____

_____

_____.

Finding a Perspective on the Process or System

- Thinking about this process or system makes me feel _____

_____

- I want anyone who reads my essay to know that _____

_____

- The best way to show my point of view is to include _____,

_____, and _____.

Identifying the Readers You Want to Reach

- My audience includes _____.

- They might be interested in this process or system because _____

_____

- They probably will not know much about _____

_____

- I need to tell this audience _____

  _____,

  so they will understand the process or system.

- I need to show this audience _____

  _____,

  so they will understand the process or system.

- When they read my essay, I want them to feel _____

  _____.

- My purpose for writing is to _____.

Finding Concrete Details to Support a Process Analysis Essay

Brainstorm as many of the following prompts as possible, identifying concrete sensory details that reinforce the ability of your readers to understand a system (in a how-it-works essay) or follow the steps of a process (in a how-to essay). What details will be most helpful in clarifying crucial parts of the system or process?

- something seen, observed, watched that is part of the process or system

  EXAMPLES: the blue litmus paper turning pink, the magician's curled fingers disguising the coin in his palm

  _____

  _____

- a sound that is part of the process or system

  EXAMPLES: the whir of sewing machines, the dog trainer's commanding tone

  _____

  _____

- an aroma, smell, or stench that relates to the process or system

  EXAMPLES: the stale smell of socks being loaded into a washer, the scent of earth in a greenhouse full of seedlings ready for transplant

  _____

  _____

- something tangible or textured that is part of the process or system

    EXAMPLES: the smooth, elastic texture of dough after kneading, the tiny meshing teeth of the gears in the clock

    _____
    _____
    _____

- a flavor or taste that connects to the process or system

    EXAMPLES: the mouth-puckering sourness of raw rhubarb, the sweet and salty taste of my favorite lemonade recipe

    _____
    _____
    _____

Finding Figures of Speech to Enliven a Process Analysis

Practice making comparisons to make an unfamiliar process or system clear to readers.

- If _____ (process or system) were a living thing, it would be _____ because _____.
- If _____ (process or system) were a _____, it would be _____ because _____.
- _____ (process or system) reminds me of _____ because _____.

- People say that _____ (process or system) is like _____, but I don't think that is true because _____.

Now try writing your own comparison.

_____
_____
_____

Illustrating a Process or System

You may find that readers of your process analysis essay need diagrams or other visuals to help them understand the process you are describing. Will your audience need such assistance? If so, where can you find — or how can you create — visuals that will be helpful?

Brainstorming the Steps in a Process

Make a list of every step that readers unfamiliar with the process or system will need to know, and then try one or more of these ideas to figure out what else you will need to include.

- Ask a friend or classmate to act out the steps as you read them. What is missing or difficult to follow?
- Ask someone to sketch the steps as you read them. Where do the instructions go wrong?
- Ask two or three classmates to listen while you read the steps, Ask them to raise their hands whenever something is not clear. Do they agree on what the problems are?

THESIS ACTIVITIES

- My preliminary topic (from p. 98) is _____.

Narrowing and Focusing a Topic for a Process Analysis Essay

Is your preliminary topic something that you can describe in an essay of the assigned length? Sometimes a narrower topic allows you to create a better process analysis.

- To me, the single most important thing about this topic is (pick one and complete the sentence)
  - that it made me realize _____.
  - that it is unique because _____.
  - that it reminds me of _____.
  - that understanding it allows me to _____.
  - that _____
    _____.

- If I had five minutes to explain why I have a strong interest in this process or system, I would start with _____
  _____.

Moving from Topic to Thesis for a Process Analysis Essay

Fill in the blanks to start thinking about making some kind of assertion about the importance or relevance of your topic to your readers.

- Many people are surprised to find out that (the process or system) is _____.

- I used to believe _____ about (the process or system), but now I think _____.

- This may sound strange, but (the process or system) reminds me of _____ because _____.

- I did not expect (the process or system) to make much of an impression on me, but _____.

- The reason audiences should care about (the process or system) is _____ _____.

- An ordinary _____ is like _____, but (this process or system) is different because _____ _____.

- Invent your own assertion about your topic.

  _____

  _____

  _____

Creating a Preliminary Thesis Statement for a Process Analysis Essay

Remember that a thesis statement needs a topic — but it also needs to make some kind of assertion about the topic. In a process analysis essay, the thesis should emphasize why readers will benefit from understanding this process or system.

- Understanding _____ (the process or system) can make your life better because _____.
- _____ (the process or system) is beneficial for _____ (audience) because _____ _____.

Reread the ideas you've come up with about your topic on pp. 97–101, and try writing a thesis statement of your own.

_____

_____

_____

DRAFTING ACTIVITIES

Deciding Where to Begin

What part of the draft are you most excited about writing or do you feel best prepared to begin? Start with that part. If you feel confident about the steps in the process but not how you want to introduce or conclude the process analysis, begin with body paragraphs. If you have an idea for a solid jumping-off place that will help you write coherent body paragraphs, begin with an introduction. You don't need to write the draft in the order it will be read; just get started.

Brainstorming Ways to Get Readers' Attention

Keeping your thesis and the steps of your process in mind, try your hand at these effective ways to start an introduction.

- a quotation (something you said, something someone said to you, a quotation from a book or film, etc.)

  _____

- an anecdote or story (something that sheds light on the process you're describing or explains how you came to realize the importance of your topic)

  _____

- a provocative statement (a surprising or shocking comparison or an unexpected revelation)

  _____

- a question that prompts readers to think about how they will answer it

  _____

- a hypothetical situation that invites others to imagine being in someone else's place

  _____

- a comparison of the process with something more familiar to readers (see p. 98) _____

Drafting an Introduction

Choose the opening you like most from the examples you've created, and start a new draft that begins with that opening. Then write the preliminary thesis that you created on p. 98. How easily can you move from a catchy opening sentence to your preliminary thesis?

1. Try to connect your opening to your thesis. Can you include background information for your readers and forecast the main idea of your essay in three sentences? Expand your introduction as needed.
2. Copy and paste your opening statement, connecting sentences, and preliminary thesis into a new document. Revising any of the sentences as needed, write a complete introductory paragraph.

Trying Options for Organizing Body Paragraphs

A process analysis essay needs a clear, logical organization. For a process with a fairly small number of steps, chronological organization is a standard approach; it typically uses one paragraph per step.

Chronological order (starting at the beginning and moving forward)

- First, _____.
- Then, _____.
- Next, _____.
- After that, _____.
- Finally, _____.

If the process is more complicated, try organizing by association. Group categories of steps, using one paragraph per category, with a topic sentence that indicates the overall category.

Associational order (grouping related sets of steps)

- One part of the process _____.
  - The first step of this part is _____.
  - The second step of this part is _____.
  - The third step is _____.
  - The fourth step is _____.

- Another part of the process _____.
  - The first step of this part is _____.
  - The second step of this part is _____.
  - The third step is _____.
- A third part of the process _____.
  - The first step of this part is _____.
  - The second step of this part is _____.
  - The third step is _____.
  - The fourth step is _____.

Try it yourself!
Topic sentence of first body paragraph: _____

_____

Steps and details to include in the paragraph:

- _____
- _____
- _____

Topic sentence of second body paragraph: _____

_____

Steps and details to include in the paragraph:

- _____
- _____
- _____

Topic sentence of third body paragraph: _____

_____

Steps and details to include in the paragraph:

- _____
- _____
- _____

(Continue until you have outlined or sketched a plan for all your body paragraphs.)

Drafting a Conclusion

Your conclusion should reinforce the idea that the process is important, remind readers of situations in which the knowledge will be useful, tell a memorable story, or otherwise indicate the value of knowing the information in the essay.

- The takeaway for readers about this process or system should be that _____.

- A story or detail that reminds readers of the importance of this process is _____.

- A reason that I chose to inform readers about this process is that _____.

Try it yourself!
Draft a conclusion that sells the value of understanding this process.

_____

_____

Creating an Intriguing Title

Your title should indicate your topic and say something about it that will interest readers. Try the following ideas to create an intriguing title that your audience will want to read.

- Alliteration: The process I am describing is _____ and some words that begin with the same sound and relate to my topic are _____.

- Groups of three: Three things I talk about in the essay are _____ _____, _____, and _____.

- Question: People ask _____ about this process.

- Quotation: Someone said "_____" about this process.

- Try out a title of your own: _____

FEEDBACK ACTIVITIES

Getting Your Questions Answered by Peer Reviewers

You'll get better feedback from peer reviewers if you ask for specific help with comments and questions like these.

- I'm not sure whether or not _____ is working.
- Does the description of _____ make sense?
- My biggest concern is _____.

Now write the question with which you *most* want your peer reviewers' help.

_____

_____

Asking Reviewers for Feedback about a Process Analysis Essay

To find out if reviewers are getting the information they need from your process analysis essay, have them answer the following questions.

- What is the thesis? How well does it explain the value of reading this essay?
- How well do the topic sentences of the body paragraphs explain what is to follow in the steps of the process?
- How well do you understand each step? What, if anything, is unclear?
- What important questions do you have that are not answered by the essay?
- What details work best for this essay? What do you like about them?
- Which details are weakest? Which ideas need further development?
- How well does the essay hang together? How effective are the transitions between paragraphs?
- How enticing is the introduction? Which parts make you want to keep reading? What is less interesting?
- How well does the conclusion end the essay? What works best to bring the essay to an end? What should change?
- How effective is the title? Why?
- My favorite part of this essay is _____

   because _____.

- The part that I think needs the most improvement is _____

   because _____.

Conducting a Self-Review

Put your draft aside for at least one day. Then, read it again, doing your best to pretend that you have never seen it before. Use the Rubric for Assessing Process Analysis Essays to rate your draft in its current form. (Your instructor may use other criteria for assessing student writing, so be sure to check with him or her about expectations.)

Rubric for Assessing Process Analysis Essays

	Exceeds expectations	Meets expectations	Needs improvement	Does not meet expectations
Focus, purpose, and audience	The essay identifies a specific process from the writer's experience or knowledge. The introduction briefly establishes the process to be analyzed, the kind of process it is, the writer's purpose for analyzing it, and the tone. A clear thesis gives purpose to the analysis and controls all development; body paragraphs analyzing steps in the process are focused by effectively governing topic sentences.	The essay addresses a process that is meaningful to the audience and appropriate to the assignment. The introduction indicates the writer's purpose and establishes a tone, but may not indicate what kind of process will be analyzed or why it might be important or interesting to the target audience. The thesis focuses all or most of the development. Body paragraphs analyze steps in the process, but topic sentences may be too narrow to effectively focus the content.	A topic is apparent but the paper may confuse process analysis with another method of development, or it may fail in some other way to satisfy the assignment's requirements. If a thesis is present, it is not analytical or is too broad to clarify the purpose or appeal to the target audience. Body paragraphs may be too short or too long, and their development is not effectively focused by topic sentence reflecting steps in the process being analyzed. Some irrelevant content may be included.	No clear thesis or analytical purpose is evident, or the paper fails to engage the reader's favorable attention. Impressions and vague abstract statements may generally relate to an identified topic but do not constitute analysis. Body paragraphs are either underdeveloped or are undifferentiated, with the paper taking the form of one long paragraph. Irrelevant material may intrude or contradictory material may confuse the reader about the paper's focus or purpose.

Feedback Activities

	Exceeds expectations	Meets expectations	Needs improvement	Does not meet expectations
Development	The essay offers well-chosen, concrete details that allow audience members to understand how the process is completed or to perform the steps themselves. All materials necessary for completing directional process analysis are listed. Instructive exposition develops each body paragraph, anticipating the readers' questions. Where appropriate, cautions or alternative means of completing each step are included. Exposition and forecasting statements offer helpful context.	Details serve to effectively engage the audience and suffice to explain how the process is completed, accomplishing the composition's analytical purpose. Content is relevant, with no disruption of essay or paragraph unity and no distortion or ambiguity about completion of either the individual steps or the process as a whole. A list of materials necessary for completing the process may be included and will be largely complete; cautions or caveats may also be included if warranted.	Details and specifics are sparse, overbalanced by general statements that tell about the process rather than relating the steps and how they occur or are completed. Descriptive or editorial observations may inappropriately constitute the bulk of the paper's development. Irrelevant observations or opinions may intrude and distract the reader or obscure the point. A list of materials may be incomplete, and steps may be missing.	Few or no details or specifics are included. General statements are vague or they distort or confuse the thesis rather than serving to validate or clarify it. No effort to offer instructions or explain how steps occur is apparent. Commentary or personal opinion is offered, but is not clearly related to an analytical purpose. No lists of materials or conditions are included, so development fails to engage or instruct the reader.
Organization and coherence	A clear chronological sequence governs development of a process at both essay and paragraph levels. Background information	Development is reasonably organized throughout, arranged to show the chronological sequencing of elements, but arrangement	Chronological organization is attempted but inconsistent. The reader can discern a sequence of steps but can only follow it with difficulty, as	The essay has no discernible organization at essay or paragraph level. Disjointed sentences fail to reflect the structure of the process being

	Exceeds expectations	Meets expectations	Needs improvement	Does not meet expectations
Organization and coherence	and forecasting statements are marked clearly with well-chosen transitional devices. Nonlinear process elements are clearly distinguished and are organized using some appropriate principle. Topic sentences of body paragraphs relate consistently to linking elements in the introduction and conclusion.	of nonlinear elements may be misrepresented as occurring in a chronological sequence as well. Background and forecasting statements are signaled with adequate transition. Transitions are adequate but may be used repetitively. Focusing statements in the introduction and conclusion help provide context. Analysis is generally coherent throughout.	exposition and explanation are inserted with little transition. Transitions are used improperly, randomly, or repetitively. The introduction and conclusion fail to provide coherence or make the analysis fully comprehensible. The writer may include statements such as "I forgot to mention." Coherence is generally weak at both essay and paragraph levels.	analyzed. No expository or explanatory content is introduced, and the essay employs inadequate or misleading transitional devices or organizational cues. No contextualizing statements are included in either introduction or conclusion; the analytical purpose is not achieved.
Style and structure	Design of introductory and body elements engage the audience's favorable attention and guide it through the essay's content, arranged in coherent body paragraphs. A conclusion sums up the steps in the process or offers commentary	The introduction identifies the process to be analyzed, establishes an appropriate tone, and guides the reader into the body of the paper, which is developed in multiple separate paragraphs. A functional conclusion is present. The writing employs	The essay uses spacing or indention, but paragraphing is weak. Introductory and concluding elements may be underdeveloped or absent entirely. Steps are not distinguished from one another by inclusion in separate, distinct paragraphs. Sentences employ	Paragraphing is absent or insufficient to meet the demands of the writing situation, with no distinct introductory or concluding elements included. Body paragraphs are either too short or the body is not organized into separate paragraphs. Sentences are difficult to

	Exceeds expectations	Meets expectations	Needs improvement	Does not meet expectations
Style and structure	reinforcing the purpose and thesis. The paper achieves variety in sentence pattern and type. Tone is skillfully controlled; word choice is apt and artful.	little variety of pattern or type, but sentence construction is competent. Diction is appropriate to audience or purpose, but may be repetitive or imprecise.	faulty or mixed constructions, with little or no variety in pattern or type. Tone and diction are inappropriate for the purpose and audience.	interpret; the writer does not demonstrate control of grammar or paragraph structure. Tone and diction are contradictory or inappropriate.
Precision and editing	The writer reveals mastery of all elements of grammar, usage, and mechanical conventions. Verb tenses are consistent, with appropriate shifts. Uses of second person perspective and passive voice are absent or appropriate. Items in lists are parallel in construction and punctuated properly. Body paragraphs representing individual steps are also parallel in construction and length. The paper is properly formatted and attractive in appearance and contains few or no careless errors.	The essay is largely free of errors in grammar, punctuation, and use of mechanical conventions, though occasional lapses occur. Inappropriate shifts in verb tense and person may occasionally be included, but do not create confusion. Listed items are parallel in construction and are generally punctuated correctly, with only minor and infrequent error. The paper is neat and clear, with formatting of manuscript conventions applied consistently. The paper satisfies the assignment with only scattered errors.	The essay is weakened with frequent errors in grammar, punctuation, and the use of mechanical conventions. Punctuation of items in lists includes frequent errors; parallelism is faulty, and shifts in verb tense and perspective are pervasive and distracting. The submission may be crumpled, stained, or torn. Errors in manuscript formatting conventions draw unfavorable attention. Numerous editing errors distract the reader, though perhaps cause little or no confusion.	Verb and pronoun usage, sentence constructions, and diction are consistently faulty. Sentence structure is dysfunctional. Punctuation is inconsistent. Careless or illegible writing is confusing. Stains, rips, blots, or printing errors distract the reader and may make parts of the paper unreadable. The writer fails to observe manuscript conventions or to satisfy other demands of the assignment. Errors throughout are serious enough to cause confusion and misunderstanding of meaning.

Gathering Responses and Collecting Your Thoughts

Gather all the reviewer responses. Make notes about what your reviewers agree and disagree on, moving from most important issues, such as thesis, organization, completeness of coverage of the process, interest, and support for ideas, to least important, such as spelling and comma placement. List areas where you agree that improvement is needed, and make a plan about what you need to revise. Think about areas of disagreement, too. You make the final decisions about what changes to make, so determine which comments you need to respond to and which you can ignore.

REVISION AND EDITING ACTIVITIES

Identifying Options for Revision Planning

After you have gathered revision comments on your early draft from peer reviewers and your instructor (pp. 106–07), choose one of the following strategies to begin making your revision plan.

- Create a storyboard. On a sticky note or note card, write your thesis statement or dominant impression, and put it at the top of your work area. Using separate sticky notes or note cards for each paragraph or example, write down important features such as topic sentences and supporting details. Does your organization make sense? Do the parts work together? Does every paragraph contribute to an understanding of the process? Using sticky notes or note cards of a different color, add notes to each paragraph about how you will strengthen, change, or delete content based on your reviewers' comments and your own. Take photos of the parts of the storyboard so you'll have a record of what you decide, even if you lose your notes.

- Create a graphic organizer. Using either paper and pencil or a digital document, create text boxes representing each introductory paragraph, body paragraph, and conclusion paragraph, and write the main idea of each paragraph in the box. Below it, leave room to revise the main idea. To the right of each main idea box, draw additional boxes for changes, additions, and deletions you have decided to make to supporting details, transitions, and other material in that paragraph.

- Make an annotated outline. Using formal complete sentences or informal phrases, make an outline that shows the current main ideas, supporting details, and organization of your draft. Using highlighters, colored pens, different colors of type, or some other method to make your changes clearly visible, annotate your outline to show the changes you plan to make to your thesis, dominant impression, organization, supporting ideas, introduction, conclusion, and so on.

- Make a plan of your own. _____
  _____
  _____
  _____
  _____

Revising a Process Analysis Essay

Following the plan you've created, write a complete revised draft. Repeat as needed until you feel that you have a solid draft that is nearly final.

Using Your Common Issues to Focus Editing of Your Process Analysis Essay

Edit for grammar, punctuation, and other common problems you have.

- The two kinds of problems that teachers or peer reviewers point out most often in my writing are _____ and _____.

- I know I sometimes struggle with _____.

Review the information in Part 3 (pp. 205–42) about the errors you have identified. Then reread your draft again, correcting any such errors and other issues that you find.

Proofreading

- Run the spell checker and carefully consider every suggestion. Do not automatically accept the suggestions! Remember that spell checkers cannot identify problems with certain kinds of words, such as homonyms and proper nouns (names), so check the spelling of such words yourself. If you keep track of the words you commonly misspell, you can improve your spelling, so consider a spelling-mistake list based on what you find.
- Read your essay aloud slowly, noting and correcting any issues that you find.
- Read your essay aloud backward, word by word, looking for repeated words and similar mistakes that are easy to miss in work that is very familiar. Correct any problems you see.

When your work is as error-free and professional as you can make it, submit your essay.

9

DEFINITION

PREWRITING ACTIVITIES

Finding Ideas for a Definition Essay Topic

An extended definition essay is a detailed explanation of the meaning of an unfamiliar term, often including multiple methods of development and addressing misconceptions about what is being defined. To identify a concept that can serve as the topic for your definition essay, try the following prompts.

- Recently, several people have asked me what _____ _____ means.

- An unfamiliar term I have encountered over and over in my _____ class is _____.

- Older people probably do not know the meaning of _____ _____.

- I call myself a _____, but that term means different things to different people. To me, it means _____.

Try it yourself!
Identify a word or phrase that you can define for an audience that is likely to be unfamiliar with it.

_____

_____

_____

Browsing for Ideas for a Definition Essay Topic

To generate ideas for the topic of a definition essay, browse for topics directly and also keep an eye out for ideas as you do your coursework and go about your daily life.

- Browse online, starting with topics that interest you and following links and resources where they take you. Keep a running list of concepts that are new to you or that you think will probably be unfamiliar to an audience you want to reach.

- Look at dictionary websites. The aggregator site onelook.com features a "word of the day" on its home page, and Merriam-Webster's online site has a sidebar for "trending words," often with links to short articles about those hot topics.

- Review your notes from other classes, and consider whether terms you learn in history or psychology might make good choices for a definition essay.

Identifying a Preliminary Topic for a Definition Essay

What general statement or concept will you define in your essay? The topic can be one that you started with on p. 114, or it can be an idea that came to you while you were exploring something else in one of the activities above.

- My preliminary topic is _____

_____

_____

Finding a Perspective on the Preliminary Topic for Your Definition Essay

In order to find examples that will work well for your definition, you should consider your point of view of the topic.

- This topic makes me feel _____

_____

- I want anyone who reads my definition essay to know that _____
  _____.
- The best way to show my point of view is to include _____,
  _____, and _____.

Identifying the Readers I Want to Reach in My Definition Essay

Figuring out what your audience already knows and does not know about the topic will be extremely important. If you consider what they already believe or actually know, you will be able to identify information that will make your definition more compelling. Complete the following prompts to analyze the audience you expect to reach.

- My audience includes _____.
- They may already know _____ about this topic, but they may not know _____
  _____.
- I need to tell this audience about _____
  _____ so they will understand my perspective on the topic.
- When they read my essay, I want them to feel _____
  _____.
- My purpose for writing is to _____.

Exploring Ideas for a Definition Essay

What do you need to explain so that your definition is clear, and do you need to seek additional information? Respond to any of the following prompts that are appropriate for your definition essay:

- I [already have/do not yet have] the information I need to complete a definition essay.
- Other resources for information for my definition essay might include _____
  _____.
- A mistaken idea that people may associate with this topic is _____
  _____.

- A visual that would clarify the topic is _____.
  My plan for including a visual is _____
  _____.

- My own experience with _____
  can help me explain it to others because _____
  _____.

Identifying Strong, Vivid Examples for a Definition Essay

Specific details make a definition come alive. Brainstorm as many of the following prompts as possible to try out other methods of development that can add interest to your definition essay.

- narrative examples

    EXAMPLE: a story about the people who originally called themselves "mugwumps"

- descriptive examples

    EXAMPLE: a detailed description of the setting for a meditation retreat

- process analysis examples

    EXAMPLE: a definition of multitasking that identifies the steps in completing a reading assignment while texting and listening to music

- causal analysis examples

    EXAMPLE: an examination of the effects of single-payer health-care systems on patients' treatment in Canada and France

- Try creating an example from any method of development that seems useful.

_____
_____
_____

Choosing Visuals or Other Media to Enliven a Definition Essay

If you have access to photos or other media that will help create a vivid impression of the concept you are defining, consider including one or more of them in your essay. Video and audio files can be used in an essay that you will post online.

THESIS ACTIVITIES

- My preliminary topic [p. 115] is _____.

Narrowing and Focusing a Topic for a Definition Essay

Will you be able to define the concept adequately in an essay of the assigned length? Sometimes a narrower, more focused topic may allow you to create a better definition essay.

- If I had five minutes to define the idea to people who are not familiar with it, I would start with _____
_____.

Identifying a Point for Your Definition Essay

To me, the single most important thing about the topic I am trying to define is (pick one and complete the sentence)

- that it clarifies _____.
- that it helps people understand _____.
- that it proves _____.
- that it is exciting because _____.
- that it is important because _____.
- that _____
_____.

Moving from Topic to Preliminary Thesis for a Definition Essay

Fill in the blanks to start thinking about the point you want to make in your definition essay.

1. Many people will be surprised to find out that _____ _____.

2. I used to believe _____, but now I think _____.

3. This may sound strange, but [the topic] makes me think about _____ because _____.

4. At first I did not understand [the topic], but now I think of it as _____ _____.

5. A new insight my readers should have about [the topic] is _____ _____.

Now, write your own generalization that can serve as a preliminary thesis.

_____
_____
_____

Testing Your Thesis

In a sentence or two, explain your proposed thesis for your definition essay to a classmate or friend who is part of your audience. Ask for responses to these questions.

- How much do you understand about the concept being defined?
  _____
  _____

- How does the plan for this definition essay seem likely to expand your understanding of the concept?
  _____
  _____

- What interests you most about this topic? Why? _____
  _____

Do the reviewers' responses suggest that you are on the right track? If not, consider whether you should rethink your topic, review your assumptions about what your audience knows and cares about, or reconsider the examples you will use.

DRAFTING ACTIVITIES

Deciding Where to Begin

Begin at the easiest point for you to get started. If starting with the dictionary definition will help you get your draft underway, begin there. If you know you want to include an image or video clip as an example, begin with that. You can start with the introduction, of course, but you do not have to begin at the beginning; you can draft the introduction and conclusion after the body of your essay if you like.

Brainstorming Ways to Get Readers' Attention

Keeping your preliminary thesis in mind, try your hand at these effective ways to start an introduction:

- a quotation (something you said, something someone said to you, a relevant snippet of dialogue that will be part of one of your examples)

  _____
  _____

- an anecdote or a story (something that sheds light on the subject you are defining or explains how you came to realize the importance of your topic)

  _____
  _____

- a provocative statement (a surprising or shocking announcement or an unexpected revelation)

  _____
  _____

- a question that prompts readers to think about how they will answer it

  _____
  _____

- a hypothetical situation that invites others to imagine being in someone else's place

  _____
  _____

- a comparison that shows how your unfamiliar concept is like something more familiar to your readers

  _____
  _____

Drafting an Introduction

Choose the opening you like most from the examples you've created, and start a new draft that begins with that opening. How can you move from this catchy opening to your first example?

Trying Options for Organizing Body Paragraphs

If you aren't certain what organization makes sense for the examples that will support your thesis, try completing any of the following options that seem viable. Use the option you choose as the basis for an outline or graphic organizer that you can follow as you draft.

By Time

- Chronological order: start at the beginning and move forward in time
- Reverse chronological order: move from most recent time to earliest

In Order of Importance, Familiarity, or Interest

- Least to most important, familiar, or interesting: save the best for last
- Most to least important, familiar, or interesting: start strong

Try it yourself!

- Organization plan for examples: _____

Topic of first body paragraph: _____

- I will develop the example(s) using the _____ method.

Details to include in the paragraph:

- _____
- _____
- _____

Topic of second body paragraph: _____

- I will develop the example(s) using the _____ method.
  Details to include in the paragraph:

    - _____
    - _____
    - _____

Topic of third body paragraph:

- I will develop the example(s) using the _____ method.
  Details to include in the paragraph:

    - _____
    - _____
    - _____

(Continue until you have outlined or sketched a plan for all of your body paragraphs.)

Drafting a Conclusion

Your conclusion should reinforce the way you have defined your concept and make a final statement.

- This definition is important because _____.
- Readers should feel _____.

Try it yourself!

Draft a conclusion that reinforces your thesis and ties the whole essay together.

_____
_____
_____

Creating an Intriguing Title

Your title should indicate the topic of your definition essay and say something about it that will interest readers. Try the following ideas to create an intriguing title that your audience will want to read:

- Alliteration: My definition relates to _____, and some words that begin with the same sound and relate to my examples are _____.

- Groups of three: Three things that are important to the definition are _____, _____, and _____.

- Question: People ask _____ _____ about this definition.

- Quotation: Someone said "_____ _____" about the topic I am defining.

- Try out a title of your own: _____

FEEDBACK ACTIVITIES

Getting Your Questions Answered by Peer Reviewers

You'll get better feedback from peer reviewers if you ask for specific help with comments and questions like these.

- I'm not sure whether or not _____ is working.
- Does the example about _____ make sense?
- My biggest concern is _____.

Now write the question with which you *most* want your peer reviewers' help.

_____
_____
_____

Asking Reviewers for Feedback about a Definition Essay

To find out if reviewers are getting the impressions you want to give in your definition essay, have them answer the following questions.

- What is the thesis? Is it interesting?
- How clearly do the examples illustrate the thesis? Which example(s) do you like best? Which do you like least?
- What questions are not answered that should be answered?
- What details work well? What do you like about them?
- Which details are weakest? Which ideas need further development?
- Does the essay's organization make sense?
- How well does the essay hang together? How effective are the transitions between paragraphs?
- How enticing is the introduction? Which parts make you want to keep reading? What is less interesting?
- How well does the conclusion end the essay? What works best to bring the essay to an end? What should change?
- How effective is the title? Why?
- My favorite part of this essay is _____

    because _____.
- The part that I think needs the most improvement is _____

    because _____.

Conducting a Self-Review

Put your draft aside for at least one day. Then, read it again, doing your best to pretend that you have never seen it before. Use the Rubric for Assessing Definition Essays to see how well you think you have accomplished the essay's objectives in this draft. (Your instructor may use other criteria for assessing student writing, so be sure to check with him or her about expectations.)

Rubric for Assessing Definition Essays

	Exceeds expectations	Meets expectations	Needs improvement	Does not meet expectations
Focus, purpose, and audience	The essay identifies a term to serve as the subject of definition, indicates the class to which it belongs (what it is a type of), and identifies the feature(s) that distinguish it from other members of its class. The writer's purpose for employing this method is clear. The introduction forecasts the supplementary modes of development that will be used to develop an extended definition. The tone is engaging to an academic audience. A clear thesis statement controls all development; body paragraphs are clearly focused by topic sentences.	The essay defines a term or concept appropriate to the assignment. The introduction clearly indicates the term, its class, and its distinguishing features, generally indicates the writer's purpose, and establishes an appropriate tone, but may not clearly establish why the paper's content or conclusions might be important or interesting to an academic audience. A thesis statement focuses all or most of the development. Body paragraphs describe the distinguishing features, but topic sentences may not sharply focus the content.	The essay addresses a subject of definition, but it may be too familiar or obvious to the audience to be engaging. The introduction may list distinguishing features but does not clearly state the class to which the subject of definition belongs. If a thesis is present, it fails to clarify the purpose or in some other way fails to focus the reader's attention. The tone does not match the purpose or is not appropriate for an academic audience. Body paragraphs may be too short or too long, and their development is not effectively focused by topic sentences. No supplementary modes of development are employed to create an extended definition.	Although a subject suitable to the assignment may be addressed in the first paragraph, no class or distinguishing features are identified, or the composition may be descriptive in nature instead of establishing a definition. Vague general statements may relate to an identified topic but do not indicate a purpose. The essay may seem to have been written to fulfill a requirement rather than to benefit a reader. Body paragraphs are underdeveloped or are undifferentiated, taking the form of one long paragraph. Irrelevant material may intrude or contradictory material may confuse the reader about the focus or purpose.

	Exceeds expectations	Meets expectations	Needs improvement	Does not meet expectations
Development	The essay provides authoritative development for each distinguishing feature and each component of the extended definition. It clearly interprets the significance of the content with respect to the identified purpose. Instructive clarifying detail or description develops each body paragraph, anticipating the readers' questions. Supplementary modes of development (i.e., description, illustration, or classification) are employed to clarify or enrich the reader's understanding of the subject of definition.	Corroborative details serve to effectively engage the audience and support the paper's thesis and topic sentences. The development is sufficient to show how the features described distinguish the subject from other members of its class, but may not show why the information is relevant to the writer's purpose or to an academic audience. All content is directly relevant to the thesis, and the development of each body paragraph clarifies the distinguishing features or contributes to the extended definition, with no disruption of essay or paragraph unity.	Development lacks specific detail and general statements or claims concerning the subject of definition and its class or distinguishing features are unsupported. Although the paper may offer a thesis statement, it fails to clearly explain how the information is useful or why an understanding of it is relevant to an academic audience, so the purpose of the essay is not fully achieved. Irrelevant observations or opinions may intrude and distract the reader or obscure the point.	If an appropriate subject of definition is identified, few or no details are included to develop the basic definition, and no extended definition is developed. General statements are vague or they distort or confuse the thesis, if one is present, rather than serving to validate or clarify it. The essay does not explain or suggest how an understanding of the subject of definition is useful or relevant to the audience, so fails to achieve any meaningful purpose. Body paragraphs are not unified, being largely comprised of impressions or statements of opinion.

	Exceeds expectations	Meets expectations	Needs improvement	Does not meet expectations
Organization and coherence	Development is logically organized, following the sequence of distinguishing features indicated in a governing thesis statement. Those features are sequenced for emphasis or according to a logical principle. Shifts from one feature to the next are clearly marked with well-chosen and artfully varied transitional expressions or brief transition paragraphs. Elements of an extended definition developed around supplementary modes of development (such as contrast, description, or process analysis) are also clearly and logically organized, so the essay is fully coherent at essay and paragraph levels.	Development is reasonably organized, generally following the sequence of distinguishing features indicated in a governing thesis statement, but no discernible organizing principle informs the sequencing of features. Elements of an extended definition are generally distinguishable from one another if present. Transitions from one distinguishing feature or extension strategy to the next are appropriately signaled; transitional expressions are employed effectively but may be used repetitively. The essay is generally coherent throughout.	Organization is attempted but inconsistent. An ineffective thesis statement fails to clearly signal the order in which body content will be presented. Individual sentences are comprehensible, but their sequencing is not clearly governed by a discernible organizing principle. Transitions are used improperly, randomly, or repetitively. Elements developing distinguishing features or extending the definition are not adequately distinguished if present, leading to some confusion. Shifts from one feature or extension component to the next are not clearly marked. Coherence is generally weak at both essay and paragraph levels.	The essay has no discernible organization at essay or paragraph level. Disjointed sentences reflect failure to systematically arrange any elements of the essay. An introduction offers no indication of the order in which body content will be introduced, and the essay employs inadequate or misleading transitional devices or organizational cues. Shifts from one distinguishing feature to the next are random. No elements of an extended definition are included or are mixed indiscriminately if present. The composition is largely incoherent throughout.

	Exceeds expectations	Meets expectations	Needs improvement	Does not meet expectations
Style and structure	Design of introductory, body, and concluding elements establish and fully develop the subject, class, and distinguishing features, engage the audience's favorable attention, and provide a map of the essay's content, arranged in coherent body paragraphs. A conclusion sums up the purpose, function, and significance of the definition offered, and reinforces the writer's purpose and thesis. The paper achieves variety in sentence pattern and type. Tone is skillfully controlled; word choice is apt, varied, and artful.	The introduction identifies a subject, class, and distinguishing features, establishes an appropriate tone, and guides the reader into the body of the paper, which is developed in multiple separate paragraphs. A functional conclusion is present. The writing employs little variety of pattern or type, but sentence construction is competent. Diction is generally appropriate to audience and purpose, but phrasing may be repetitive or imprecise.	The essay uses spacing or indention, but paragraphing is weak. Introductory and concluding elements may be underdeveloped or absent entirely. Development of distinguishing features is delineated in separate, distinct paragraphs. Sentences employ faulty or mixed constructions, with little or no variety in pattern or type. Tone and diction lapse into inappropriate informality or stiffness.	Paragraphing is absent or insufficient to meet the demands of the writing situation, with no distinct introductory or concluding elements included. Body paragraphs are either too short or the body is not organized into separate paragraphs. Sentences are difficult to interpret; the writer does not demonstrate control of grammar or paragraph structure. Tone and diction are contradictory or inappropriate.
Precision and editing	The writer reveals mastery of all elements of grammar, usage, and mechanical conventions. Verb tenses are consistent, with appropriate shifts in passages of	The essay is largely free of errors in grammar, punctuation, and use of mechanical conventions, though occasional lapses occur. Verb tenses	The essay is weakened with frequent errors in grammar, punctuation, and the use of mechanical conventions. Shifts in verb tense and	Verb and pronoun usage, sentence constructions, and diction are consistently faulty. Sentence structure is dysfunctional. Punctuation is arbitrary. Careless or illegible writing

	Exceeds expectations	Meets expectations	Needs improvement	Does not meet expectations
Precision and editing	transition and forecasting. Uses of second person perspective and passive voice are appropriate if present. The paper is properly formatted and attractive in appearance and contains few or no careless errors. Overall the composition is memorable and exemplary.	may shift, and inappropriate shifts in person may occasionally be included, but do not create confusion. The paper is neat, legible, and clear, with formatting of manuscript conventions applied consistently. The paper satisfies the assignment with only scattered careless errors.	perspective are pervasive and distracting. The submission may be crumpled, stained, or torn. Errors in manuscript formatting conventions draw unfavorable attention. Numerous careless errors distract the reader, though perhaps cause little or no confusion.	is confusing. Stains, rips, blots, or printing errors distract the reader and may make parts of the paper illegible. The writer fails to observe manuscript conventions or to satisfy other demands of the assignment. Errors throughout are serious enough to cause confusion and misunderstanding.

Gathering Responses and Collecting Your Thoughts

Gather all the reviewer responses. Make notes about what you and your reviewers agree and disagree on, moving from most important issues, such as appropriateness of the topic, the effectiveness of the examples, the organization, and the support for ideas, to least important, such as spelling and comma placement. List areas where you agree that improvement is needed, and make a plan about what you need to revise. Think about areas of disagreement, too. You make the final decisions about what changes to make, so determine which comments you need to respond to and which you can ignore.

REVISION AND EDITING ACTIVITIES

Identifying Options for Revision Planning

After you have gathered revision comments on your early draft from peer reviewers and your instructor (pp. 123–24), choose one of the following strategies to begin making your revision plan.

- Create a storyboard. On a sticky note or note card, write the term you are defining and put it at the top of your work area. Using separate sticky notes or note cards for each paragraph or example, write down important features such as topic sentences and supporting details. Does your organization make sense? Do the parts work together? Does every paragraph help to advance the definition and clarify the point the essay makes? Using sticky notes or note cards of a different color, add notes to each paragraph about how you will strengthen, change, or delete content based on your reviewers' comments and your own. Take photos of the parts of the storyboard so you'll have a record of what you decide, even if you lose your notes.

- Create a graphic organizer. Using either paper and pencil or a digital document, create text boxes representing each introductory paragraph, body paragraph, and conclusion paragraph, and write the main idea of each paragraph in the box. Below it, leave room to revise the main idea. To the right of each main idea box, draw additional boxes for changes, additions, and deletions you have decided to make to supporting details, transitions, and other material in that paragraph.

- Make an annotated outline. Using formal complete sentences or informal phrases, make an outline that shows the current main ideas, supporting details, and organization of your draft. Using highlighters, colored pens, different colors of type, or some other method to make your changes clearly visible, annotate your outline to show the changes you plan to make to your thesis, dominant impression, organization, supporting ideas, introduction, conclusion, and so on.

- Make a plan of your own. _____
  _____
  _____
  _____
  _____

Revising a Definition Essay

Following the plan you've created, write a complete revised draft. Repeat as needed until you feel that you have a solid draft that is nearly final.

Using Your Common Issues to Focus Editing of Your Definition Essay

Edit for grammar, punctuation, and other common problems you have.

- The two kinds of problems that teachers or peer reviewers point out most often in my writing are _____ and _____.

- I know I sometimes struggle with _____.

Review the information in Part 3 (pp. 205–42) about the errors you have identified above. Then reread your draft again, correcting any such errors and other issues that you find.

Proofreading

- Run the spell-checker and carefully consider every suggestion. Do not automatically accept the suggestions! Remember that spell-checkers cannot identify problems with certain kinds of words, such as homonyms and proper nouns (names), so check the spelling of such words yourself. Write the words you have misspelled on a spelling checklist you can use to identify and avoid words that give you trouble.

- Read your essay aloud slowly, noting and correcting any issues that you find.

- Read your essay aloud backward, word by word, looking for repeated words and similar mistakes that are easy to miss in work that is very familiar. Correct any problems you see.

When your work is as error-free and professional as you can make it, submit your essay.

10

DIVISION AND CLASSIFICATION

PREWRITING ACTIVITIES

Getting Started with a Division and Classification Topic

Complete as many of the following prompts as you can to start thinking about topics for an essay that analyzes the parts that make up a whole, or the categories into which members of a group may be divided.

- Every _____ is either _____, _____, or _____.
- The class is made up of the following kinds of students: _____, _____, _____, and _____. Which one are you?
- The idea of _____ can seem overwhelming until you realize that you can break it down into manageable parts.

- There are [two/three/four] types of _____:
  _____, _____,
  _____, and _____.

Now try one of your own:

_____

_____

_____

Freewriting to Generate Ideas for a Division and Classification Essay

Work with a classmate to decide on a broad general category (internet memes, movies featuring a particular star, restaurants near campus, classes or majors, etc.). Then spend five minutes brainstorming to name everything that you can think of that fits into the category, writing down all the responses. When you finish, freewrite for two minutes about ways to classify and group the elements you have named, aiming to avoid overlap between groups. Have you covered every group that is part of the category you chose?

Using Social Media to Brainstorm Classification Options

Start with a search engine such as Google and enter a phrase such as "four types of" or "three kinds of" into the search bar. Scroll through the first two pages of results. Make notes about interesting or amusing content you find that suggests ideas for your own division and classification essay.

Identifying a Useful Preliminary Topic for a Division and Classification Essay

Which category or parts of a whole seem like a good preliminary topic for a division and classification essay? The topic can be one that you started with on this page, or it can be a different idea.

- My preliminary topic is _____

_____

_____.

Finding a Perspective on What You Will Compare and Contrast

Respond to the following prompts to begin thinking about your point of view for the division and classification essay.

- I am interested in this topic because it _____.
- This topic could be amusing if _____.
- I want anyone who reads my essay to understand that _____ _____.
- The best way to show my point of view is to include _____, _____, and _____.

Identifying the Readers You Want to Reach

- My audience includes _____.
- They might be interested in this division and classification topic because _____.
- They probably will not know much about _____ _____.
- I need to tell this audience _____ so they will understand what I am discussing.
- When they read my essay, I want them to feel _____ _____.
- My purpose for writing is to _____.

Finding Concrete Details to Support a Division and Classification Essay

Brainstorm as many of the following prompts as possible, identifying concrete sensory details that reinforce the ability of your readers to understand the subgroups you are classifying or the whole that is made up of the parts. What details will be most helpful?

- something seen, observed, watched that is part of the class or group
    EXAMPLES: the clothing styles of the 1980s

_____
_____
_____

- a sound that relates to the class as a whole or to a part or subgroup

    EXAMPLES: the rattle of the dice rolled by Dungeons and Dragons players

    _____
    _____

- an aroma, smell, or stench that is relevant to the class or a subgroup

    EXAMPLES: the multiple aromas wafted around the food court by competing fast-food restaurants

    _____
    _____

- something tangible or textured that is part of the class as a whole or a subgroup

    EXAMPLES: venetian blinds, sheer gauzy curtains, vinyl roller shades, and heavy, lined drapes that cover windows in public areas of the residence hall

    _____
    _____

- a flavor or taste that connects to the class or a subgroup

    EXAMPLES: the sweet, salty, sour, bitter, and umami taste receptors on the tongue

    _____
    _____

Finding Figures of Speech to Enliven a Division and Classification Essay

Using figurative language that makes comparisons can help to clarify the categories and subgroups for readers of your division and classification essay.

- If _____ [a class] were a living thing, it would be _____

    because _____.

- If _____ [the subgroups that the class is made up of] are like [types of cars/food groups/sports], [one subgroup] would be like _____, [another subgroup] would be like _____, and [another subgroup] would be like _____.

- People say that _____ [a category] is like _____, but I don't think that is true because _____ _____.

Now try writing your own figure of speech to clarify information about the category you are describing or the subgroups of which it is composed:

_____
_____
_____

THESIS ACTIVITIES

- My preliminary topic (from p. 133) is _____.

Narrowing and Focusing a Topic for a Division and Classification Essay

Is your preliminary topic something that you can describe in an essay of the assigned length? Sometimes a narrower topic allows you to focus attention more effectively on the most relevant aspects of your classification.

- To me, the single most important thing about this class and the subgroups of which it is composed is (pick one and complete the sentence)
  - that it made me realize _____.
  - that it is meaningful because _____.
  - that it helped me decide _____.
  - that _____ _____.

- If I had five minutes to explain why I have a strong interest in making this comparison, I would start with _____ _____.

Moving from Topic to Thesis for a Division and Classification Essay

Fill in the blanks to start thinking about making some kind of assertion about the importance or relevance of your topic to your readers.

- Many people are surprised to find out that [some part of the overall class] is _____.

- I used to believe _____ about [the class or one or more subgroups], but now I think _____.

- This may sound strange, but [the class or one or more subgroups] reminds me of _____.

- I did not expect [the class or subgroup] to make much of an impression on me, but _____.

- The reason audiences should care about [the classification] is _____.

Invent your own assertion about your topic:

_____
_____
_____

Creating a Preliminary Thesis Statement for a Division and Classification Essay

Remember that a thesis statement needs a topic — but it also needs to make some kind of assertion about the topic. In a division and classification essay, the thesis should make a point about the importance of the topic so readers will understand why you are creating your essay.

- Classifying how _____ [category] is made up of _____ _____ [subcategories] reveals important ways that the class as a whole is _____.

- Understanding the types of _____ [the parts that make up the whole] is useful because _____ _____.

Reread the ideas you've come up with about your topic on pp. 132–36, and try writing a thesis statement of your own.

___

___

___

DRAFTING ACTIVITIES
Deciding Where to Begin

What part of the draft are you most excited about writing or do you feel best prepared to begin? Start with that part. If you feel confident talking about the points you want to make about the class as a whole but not about the parts, start with the section about which you have more to say. If you have an idea for a solid jumping-off place, you can begin with an introduction. You don't need to write the draft in the order it will be read; just get started.

Brainstorming Ways to Get Readers' Attention

Keeping your thesis and the steps of your process in mind, try your hand at these effective ways to start an introduction.

- a quotation (something you said, something someone said to you, a quotation from a book or film, etc.)

   ___

- an anecdote or story (something that sheds light on the classification you're addressing or explains how you came to realize the importance of your topic)

   ___

- a provocative statement (a surprising or shocking fact about the division or classification or an unexpected revelation)

   ___

- a question that prompts readers to think about how they will answer it

   ___

- a hypothetical situation that invites others to imagine being in someone else's place

   ___

- a comparison that aligns what you are writing about with something more familiar to readers (see p. 134)

Drafting an Introduction

Choose the opening you like most from the examples you've created, and start a new draft that begins with that opening. Then write the preliminary thesis that you created on p. 138. How easily can you move from a catchy opening sentence to your preliminary thesis?

1. Try to connect your opening to your thesis in four sentences or fewer. Be sure to introduce the class of subjects and give an overview of the subdivisions that you will discuss. Clarify whether you will focus on the category as a whole or on the subcategories.

2. Copy and paste your opening statement, connecting sentences, and preliminary thesis into a new document. Revising any of the sentences as needed, write a complete introductory paragraph or paragraphs.

Trying Options for Organizing Body Paragraphs

If you aren't certain what organization makes sense for the examples that will support your thesis, try completing any of the following options that seems viable. Use the option you choose as the basis for an outline or graphic organizer that you can follow as you draft.

By Time
Chronological order (starting at the beginning and moving forward)

- First, _____.
- Then, _____.
- Finally, _____.

Out of order (flashback or arrangement by association)

- A little while ago, _____.
- Before that, _____.
- Now, _____.

In Order of Importance, Familiarity, or Interest

Least to most important, familiar, or interesting (saving the best for last)

- Least _____.
- More _____.
- Most _____.

Most to least important, familiar, or interesting (starting strong)

- Most _____.
- Less _____.
- Least _____.

In Spatial Order

Moving around an object or a physical space

- On the right, _____.
- At the front, _____.
- On the left, _____.
- At the back, _____.

Try it yourself!

Topic sentence of first body paragraph: _____

　　Details to include in the paragraph:

- _____
- _____
- _____

Topic sentence of second body paragraph: _____

　　Details to include in the paragraph:

- _____
- _____
- _____

Topic sentence of third body paragraph: _____

Details to include in the paragraph:

- _____
- _____
- _____

(Continue until you have outlined or sketched a plan for all your body paragraphs.)

Drafting a Conclusion

Your conclusion should reinforce the idea that you have an important reason for writing the essay.

- The takeaway for readers should be that _____
  _____.
- The new perspective I am offering is that _____
  _____.

Try it yourself!
Draft a conclusion that clarifies the importance of your classification.

_____
_____

Creating an Intriguing Title

Your title should indicate your topic and say something about it that will interest readers. Try the following ideas to create an intriguing title that your audience will want to read.

- Alliteration: Words that start with the same sound and that relate to the classification or the subgroups are _____
  _____
- Groups of three: Three things I talk about in the essay are _____
  _____, _____,
  _____ and _____.
- Question: People ask _____
  _____ about the subjects of my division and classification essay.

- Quotation: Someone said "_____
  _____" about
  the subjects of my division and classification essay.

- Try out a title of your own: _____

FEEDBACK ACTIVITIES

Getting Your Questions Answered by Peer Reviewers

You'll get better feedback from peer reviewers if you ask for specific help with comments and questions like these.

- I'm not sure whether or not _____ is working.
- Does the description of _____ make sense?
- My biggest concern is _____.

Now write the question with which you *most* want your peer reviewers' help.

_____

_____

Asking Reviewers for Feedback about a Division and Classification Essay

To find out if reviewers are getting the information they need from your division and classification essay, have them answer the following questions.

- What is the thesis? How well does it explain the value of reading this essay?
- Is the subject interesting and compelling? Why or why not?
- How well does the organization work to convey the aspects of the subjects that are being classified and divided?
- What, if anything, is unclear? What important questions do you have that are not answered by the essay?
- What details work best for this essay? What do you like about them?
- Which details are weakest? Which ideas need further development?
- How well does the essay hang together? How effective are the transitions between paragraphs?
- How enticing is the introduction? Which parts make you want to keep reading? What is less interesting?

- How well does the conclusion end the essay? What works best to bring the essay to an end? What should change?
- How effective is the title? Why?
- My favorite part of this essay is _____

    because _____.
- The part that I think needs the most improvement is _____

    because _____.

Conducting a Self-Review

Put your draft aside for at least one day. Then, read it again, doing your best to pretend that you have never seen it before. Use the Rubric for Assessing Division and Classification Essays to rate your draft in its current form. (Your instructor may use other criteria for assessing student writing, so be sure to check with him or her about expectations.)

Rubric for Assessing Division and Classification Essays

	Exceeds expectations	Meets expectations	Needs improvement	Does not meet expectations
Focus, purpose, and audience	The essay identifies a subject of division or classification, establishes a dividing or classifying principle, and identifies categories or parts that result from applying the principle to the subject. The essay demonstrates how the system can be useful for sorting or for identifying the subject's	The essay addresses a division or classification topic that is appropriate to the assignment. The introduction clearly indicates whether the essay will divide, classify, or both. It also identifies the subject's principle and categories or parts, generally indicates the writer's purpose, and establishes	The essay addresses a subject of division or classification, but it may be too familiar or obvious to the audience to be engaging. The introduction may list categories or parts but does not clearly state the dividing or classifying principle, or it may fail in some other way to satisfy	Although a subject suitable to the assignment may be addressed in the first paragraph, no dividing or classifying principle is identified and categories or component parts are not listed systematically, or the composition may be comparative in nature instead of classifying

	Exceeds expectations	Meets expectations	Needs improvement	Does not meet expectations
	component parts. The writer's purpose for employing this mode of development is clear. The tone reflects the target audience's profile and the introduction forecasts content or conclusions that will engage the reader. A clear thesis statement controls all development; body paragraphs are clearly focused by topic sentences addressing classes or components.	an appropriate tone, but may not clearly indicate how the division or classification system is useful or important or suggest why the content or conclusions might be interesting to the target audience. A thesis statement focuses all or most of the development, but may not engage and focus the reader's attention. Body paragraphs illustrate the contents of the categories or describe the component parts, but topic sentences may not sharply focus the content.	the assignment's requirements. If a thesis is present, it fails to clarify the purpose of either the system or the essay, or both, or in some other way fails to clearly focus the reader's attention. The tone does not match the purpose or is not appropriate for the target audience. Body paragraphs may not be effectively focused by topic sentences describing the contents of the categories or the component elements of the subject. The writing may drift off topic.	or dividing as stipulated by the assignment. Impressions and vague abstract statements may generally relate to an identified topic but do not list or describe categories or components. Body paragraphs are unfocused and may be undifferentiated, with the paper taking the form of one long paragraph. Irrelevant material may intrude or contradictory material may confuse the reader about the paper's focus or purpose.
Development	The essay provides comprehensive development for each category or component of the subject and clearly interprets the significance of the content with respect to the identified purpose. Instructive	Details engage the audience and support the thesis and topic sentences. The development is sufficient to show how the categories or components are distinguished according to the	Development lacks specific detail, and general statements or claims concerning the subject of division or classification and its classes or component parts are unsupported. Although it may	If a subject of classification is identified, few or no details are included to develop categories or describe components. General statements are vague or they confuse the thesis,

Feedback Activities

	Exceeds expectations	**Meets expectations**	**Needs improvement**	**Does not meet expectations**
Development	clarifying detail or description develops each body paragraph, anticipating the readers' questions. Where appropriate, supplementary modes of development are employed to clarify or enrich the reader's understanding of the subjects.	dividing or classifying principle, but may not show how the system is useful or why it is relevant to the writer's purpose or to the reader. All content is directly relevant to the thesis, and the development of each body paragraph relates to its topic sentence, with no disruption of essay or paragraph unity.	imply a principle, the essay fails to clearly explain how the system is useful or why an understanding of it is relevant to the reader, so the purpose is not fully achieved. Irrelevant observations or opinions may intrude and distract the reader or obscure the point.	if one is present, rather than serving to validate or clarify it. No division or classification principle is identified, and the paper does not explain how the system works or is useful, or how it is relevant to the audience, so it fails to achieve any meaningful purpose. Body paragraphs are not unified, being largely constituted of impressions or statements of opinion.
Organization and coherence	Development is logically organized, following the sequence indicated in a thesis statement. The order in which categories or components are addressed is organized for emphasis or according to some other discernible organizing principle. If both division and classification elements	Development is reasonably organized, generally following the sequence of categories or components indicated in a governing thesis statement, but no discernible organizing principle informs the sequencing of body paragraphs. Division and classification elements are generally	Organization is attempted but inconsistent. An ineffective thesis statement fails to clearly signal the order in which body content will be presented. Individual sentences are comprehensible, but their sequencing is not governed by a discernible organizing principle. Transitions are	The essay has no discernible organization at essay or paragraph level. Disjointed sentences reflect failure to systematically arrange any elements of the essay. An introduction offers no indication of the order in which body content will be introduced, and the essay employs inadequate

	Exceeds expectations	Meets expectations	Needs improvement	Does not meet expectations
	are included, passages are clearly distinguished. Shifts are clearly marked with well-chosen transitions. Passages developed around supplementary modes of development are also organized appropriately, so the writing is fully coherent at essay and paragraph levels.	distinguishable from one another, if both are present. Transitions from one category or component to the next are appropriately signaled; transitional expressions are employed effectively but may be used repetitively. The essay is generally coherent throughout.	used improperly, randomly, or repetitively. Division and classification elements are not distinguished if both are present, leading to confusion. Shifts from one category or component to the next are not clearly marked. Coherence is generally weak at both essay and paragraph levels.	or misleading transitional devices or organizational cues. Shifts from one category or component to the next are unsignaled. Division and classification elements are mixed indiscriminately if both are present. The composition is largely incoherent throughout.
Style and structure	Design of introductory and body elements establish and fully develop the subject, principle, and categories of division or classification, engage the audience's favorable attention, and provide a map of the essay's content, arranged in coherent body paragraphs. A conclusion sums up the purpose, function and significance of the system and reinforces the	The introduction identifies a subject, principle, and categories or components of division or classification, establishes an appropriate tone, and guides the reader into the body of the paper, which is developed in multiple separate paragraphs. A functional conclusion is present. The writing employs little variety of pattern or type, but sentence	The essay uses spacing or indention, but paragraphing is weak. Introductory and concluding elements may be underdeveloped or absent entirely. Categories or components are not distinguished from one another by inclusion in separate, distinct paragraphs. Sentences employ faulty or mixed constructions, with little or no variety in pattern or type. Tone and	Paragraphing is absent or insufficient to meet the demands of the writing situation, with no distinct introductory or concluding elements included. Body paragraphs are either too short or the body is not organized into separate paragraphs. Sentences are difficult to interpret; the writer does not demonstrate control of

	Exceeds expectations	**Meets expectations**	**Needs improvement**	**Does not meet expectations**
Style and structure	writer's purpose and thesis. The paper achieves variety in sentence pattern and type. Tone is skillfully controlled; word choice is apt, varied, and artful.	construction is competent. Diction is generally appropriate to the audience and purpose, but phrasing may be repetitive or imprecise.	diction lapse into inappropriate informality or stiffness.	grammar or paragraph structure. Tone and diction are contradictory or inappropriate.
Precision and editing	The writer reveals mastery of all elements of grammar, usage, and mechanical conventions. Verb tenses are consistent, with appropriate shifts in passages of transition and forecasting. Uses of second person perspective and passive voice are absent or appropriate. Paragraphs treating parallel categories or components are parallel in construction and length. The paper is properly formatted and attractive in appearance, and contains few or no careless errors. Overall the composition is memorable and exemplary.	The essay is largely free of errors in grammar, punctuation, and use of mechanical conventions, though occasional lapses occur. Inappropriate shifts may occasionally occur but do not create confusion. Passages are punctuated competently, with only minor and infrequent error. The paper is neat, legible, and clear, with formatting of manuscript conventions applied consistently. The paper satisfies the assignment with only scattered editing errors.	The essay is weakened with frequent errors in grammar, punctuation, and the use of mechanical conventions. Parallelism is faulty, and inappropriate shifts in verb tense and perspective are pervasive and distracting. The submission may be crumpled, stained, or torn. Errors in manuscript formatting conventions draw unfavorable attention. Numerous careless errors distract the reader, though perhaps cause little or no confusion.	Verb and pronoun usage, sentence constructions, and diction are consistently faulty. Sentence structure is dysfunctional. Punctuation is not consistent with established conventions. Careless or illegible writing is confusing. Stains, rips, blots, or printing errors distract the reader and may make parts of the paper illegible. The writer fails to observe manuscript conventions or to satisfy other demands of the assignment. Errors throughout are serious enough to cause confusion and misunderstanding.

Gathering Responses and Collecting Your Thoughts

Gather all the reviewer responses. Make notes about what your reviewers agree and disagree on, moving from most important issues, such as thesis, organization, completeness of the groupings, interest, and support for ideas, to least important, such as spelling and comma placement. List areas where you agree that improvement is needed, and make a plan about what you need to revise. Think about areas of disagreement, too. You make the final decisions about what changes to make, so determine which comments you need to respond to and which you can ignore.

REVISION AND EDITING ACTIVITIES

Identifying Options for Revision Planning

After you have gathered revision comments on your early draft from peer reviewers and your instructor (pp. 142–43), choose one of the following strategies to begin making your revision plan.

- Create a storyboard. On a sticky note or note card, write the main point you are making as you classify and divide your subjects and put it at the top of your work area. Using separate sticky notes or note cards for each paragraph or example, write down important features such as topic sentences and supporting details. Does your organization make sense? Do the parts work together? Does every paragraph help to support the division or classification? Using sticky notes or note cards of a different color, add notes to each paragraph about how you will strengthen, change, or delete content based on your reviewers' comments and your own. Take photos of the parts of the storyboard so you'll have a record of what you decide, even if you lose your notes.

- Create a graphic organizer. Using either paper and pencil or a digital document, create text boxes representing each introductory paragraph, body paragraph, and conclusion paragraph, and write the main idea of each paragraph in the box. Below it, leave room to revise the main idea. To the right of each main idea box, draw additional boxes for changes, additions, and deletions you have decided to make to supporting details, transitions, and other material in that paragraph.

- Make an annotated outline. Using formal complete sentences or informal phrases, make an outline that shows the current main ideas, supporting details, and organization of your draft. Using highlighters, colored pens, different colors of type, or some other method to make your changes clearly visible, annotate your outline to show the changes you plan to make to your thesis, dominant impression, organization, supporting ideas, introduction, conclusion, and so on.

- Make a plan of your own. _____
  _____
  _____
  _____
  _____

Revising a Division and Classification Essay

Following the plan you've created, write a complete revised draft. Repeat as needed until you feel that you have a solid draft that is nearly final.

Using Your Common Issues to Focus Editing of Your Division and Classification Essay

Edit for grammar, punctuation, and other common problems you have.

- The two kinds of problems that teachers or peer reviewers point out most often in my writing are _____ and _____
  _____
  _____.
- I know I sometimes struggle with _____.

Review the information in Part 3 (pp. 205–42) about the errors you have identified above. Then reread your draft again, correcting any such errors and any other issues that you find.

Proofreading

- Run the spell-checker and carefully consider every suggestion. Do not automatically accept the suggestions! Remember that spell-checkers cannot identify problems with certain kinds of words, such as homonyms and proper nouns (names), so check the spelling of such words yourself. If you keep track of the words you commonly misspell, you can improve your spelling, so consider a spelling-mistake list based on what you find.
- Read your essay aloud slowly, noting and correcting any issues that you find.
- Read your essay aloud backward, word by word, looking for repeated words and similar mistakes that are easy to miss in work that is very familiar. Correct any problems you see.

When your work is as error-free and professional as you can make it, submit your essay.

11

COMPARISON AND CONTRAST

PREWRITING ACTIVITIES

Getting Started with a Comparison-and-Contrast Topic

Complete as many of the following prompts as you can to start thinking about topics for an essay that analyzes the similarities and differences between two objects, activities, places, people, or other comparable things. Comparison focuses on similarities, and contrast focuses on differences. Most comparison-and-contrast essays will emphasize either similarities or differences rather than discussing both equally.

- I need to buy a _____, and I have narrowed the choices down to _____ and _____.
- Because I enjoy _____, people often think I will also enjoy _____, but I don't.
- Two well-known people I admire who are both _____ are _____ and _____.
- The "culture clash" [in my family/among my friends] involves those who _____ and those who _____.

- The biggest change in my views on _____ since _____ [time period] is that I used to feel _____, but now I feel _____.

- If I could go anywhere I wanted on vacation, it would be difficult for me to choose between _____ and _____.

Now try one of your own.

_____

_____

_____

Brainstorming Ideas for a Comparison-and-Contrast Essay

Working with two or three classmates, decide on a general category for comparison and contrast (music, films, local restaurants, etc.) and spend five minutes calling out everything that you can think of that fits the category. Write down any ideas that seem interesting. When you finish, select two subjects from the list of ideas you have jotted down, and freewrite for two minutes about the characteristics they have in common, then for two more minutes on ways that they differ.

Identifying a Useful Preliminary Topic for a Comparison-and-Contrast Essay

Which two places, people, ideas, activities, or things seem like a good preliminary topic for a comparison-and-contrast essay? The topic can be one that you started with on this page, or it can be a different idea.

- My preliminary topic is _____

_____

_____.

Finding a Perspective on What You Will Compare and Contrast

Respond to the following prompts to begin thinking about your point of view for the comparison-and-contrast essay.

- Of the two subjects I will compare, I have [a slight/a strong/no] preference for _____.

- I want anyone who reads my essay to understand that _____

_____.

- The best way to show my point of view is to include _____, _____, and _____.

Identifying the Readers You Want to Reach

- My audience includes _____.
- They might be interested in this comparison and contrast because _____.

- They probably will not know much about _____.

- I need to tell this audience _____,
  so they will understand points of similarity and difference.
- When they read my essay, I want them to feel _____.

- My purpose for writing is to _____.

Finding Concrete Details to Support a Comparison-and-Contrast Essay

Brainstorm as many of the following prompts as possible, identifying concrete sensory details that reinforce the ability of your readers to understand the subjects you are comparing and contrasting. What details will be most helpful in clarifying similarities and differences?

- something seen, observed, watched that is part of the comparison or contrast

  EXAMPLES: Bookman serif typeface and Helvetica sans serif typeface for signage

- a sound that relates to one or both of the subjects being compared

  EXAMPLES: the garage-band production of the band's first album, the lush, layered studio sound of their second album

- an aroma, a smell, or a stench that is relevant to one or both of the subjects being compared

    EXAMPLES: the new-car smell that may or may not be worth the extra cost of a new car

    _____
    _____
    _____

- something tangible or textured that is part of one or both subjects being compared

    EXAMPLES: the hard steel taps on the sole of a tap shoe, the flexible leather sole of a jazz shoe

    _____
    _____
    _____

- a flavor or taste that connects to one or both subjects being compared

    EXAMPLES: cumin seeds fried in ghee, mustard seeds fried in oil

    _____
    _____
    _____

Finding Figures of Speech to Enliven a Comparison and Contrast

Using figurative language ("my mother's books are like pristine museum pieces on display, and my father's are worn and bedraggled like a child's favorite toys") can clarify the subjects of your comparison-and-contrast essay to help readers grasp some ideas more easily.

- If _____ [one subject in the comparison-and-contrast essay] were a living thing, it would be _____

    _____

    because _____.

- If _____ [one subject] is like a _____, then _____ [other subject] is like a _____.

- People seem to believe that _____ is very much like _____, but I don't think that is true because _____

    _____.

Now try writing your own figure of speech to clarify information about one or both of the subjects in your comparison.

_____

_____

_____

THESIS ACTIVITIES

- My preliminary topic (from p. 151) is _____.

Narrowing and Focusing a Topic for a Comparison-and-Contrast Essay

Is your preliminary topic something that you can describe in an essay of the assigned length? Sometimes a narrower topic allows you to focus attention more effectively on the most relevant aspects of your comparison.

- To me, the single most important thing about this comparison is (pick one and complete the sentence)
  - that it made me realize _____.
  - that it is meaningful because _____.
  - that it helped me decide _____.
  - that _____
    _____

- If I had five minutes to explain why I have a strong interest in making this comparison, I would start with _____
  _____.

Moving from Topic to Thesis for a Comparison-and-Contrast Essay

Fill in the blanks to start thinking about making some kind of assertion about the importance or relevance of your topic to your readers.

- Many people are surprised to find out that [some aspect of the comparison] is _____.

- I used to believe _____ about [the two subjects being compared], but now I think _____.

- This may sound strange, but [one of the subjects being compared] reminds me of _____, and the other reminds me of _____.

- I did not expect [one of the subjects being compared] to make much of an impression on me, but _____.
- The reason audiences should care about [the comparison] is _____ _____.
- Invent your own assertion about your topic.

_____
_____
_____

Creating a Preliminary Thesis Statement for a Comparison-and-Contrast Essay

Remember that a thesis statement needs a topic — but it also needs to make some kind of assertion about the topic. In a comparison-and-contrast essay, the thesis should make a point so readers will understand why you are making this comparison.

- Comparing _____ and _____ reveals important differences that matter because _____.
- _____ [one subject being compared] is beneficial for _____ [audience] because _____ _____.

Reread the ideas you've come up with about your topic on pp. 150–54, and try writing a thesis statement of your own.

_____
_____
_____

DRAFTING ACTIVITIES

Deciding Where to Begin

What part of the draft are you most excited about writing or do you feel best prepared to begin? Start with that part. If you have an idea for a solid jumping-off place, you can begin with an introduction, but you don't need to write the draft in the order it will be read; just get started.

Brainstorming Ways to Get Readers' Attention

Keeping your thesis and the steps of your process in mind, try your hand at these effective ways to start an introduction:

- a quotation [something you said, something someone said to you, a quotation from a book or film, etc.]

- an anecdote or story [something that sheds light on the comparison you're making or explains how you came to realize the importance of your topic]

- a provocative statement [a surprising or shocking fact about the comparison or an unexpected revelation]

- a question that prompts readers to think about how they will answer it

- a hypothetical situation that invites others to imagine being in someone else's place

- a comparison that aligns what you are writing about with something more familiar to readers (see p. 152)

Drafting an Introduction

Choose the opening you like most from the examples you've created, and start a new draft that begins with that opening. Then write the preliminary thesis that you created on p. 155. How easily can you move from a catchy opening sentence to your preliminary thesis?

1. Try to connect your opening to your thesis in four sentences or fewer. Be sure to introduce both things you will compare, and try to indicate a general overview of what your essay will say.

2. Copy and paste your opening statement, connecting sentences, and preliminary thesis into a new document. Revising any of the sentences as needed, write a complete introductory paragraph or paragraphs.

Trying Options for Organizing Body Paragraphs

A comparison-and-contrast essay is usually organized in one of two ways: either point by point or subject by subject.

A point-by-point organization addresses one aspect of one subject being discussed, then a related aspect of the other subject; another aspect of the first subject, then a related aspect of the second; and so on.

Point-by-point order (comparing an aspect of one subject, then a related aspect of the other subject)

- The first point of comparison for subject A _____

- The first point of comparison for subject B _____

- The second point of comparison for subject A _____

- The second point of comparison for subject B _____

- The third point of comparison for subject A _____

- The third point of comparison for subject B _____

A subject-by-subject comparison-and-contrast essay covers all aspects of the first subject being discussed before covering all the aspects of the second subject.

Subject-by-subject order (discussing all the points of comparison and contrast for one subject, then all the points for the second subject)

- The first point of comparison for subject A _____

- The second point of comparison for subject A _____

- The third point of comparison for subject A _____

- The first point of comparison for subject B _____

- The second point of comparison for subject B _____

- The third point of comparison for subject B _____

Try it yourself!

Topic sentence of first body paragraph: _____

_____.

Details about the subject and the point of comparison:

- _____
- _____
- _____

Topic sentence of second body paragraph: _____
_____.

Details about the subject and the point of comparison:

- _____
- _____
- _____

Topic sentence of third body paragraph: _____
_____.

Details about the subject and the point of comparison:

- _____
- _____
- _____

Topic sentence of fourth body paragraph: _____
_____.

Details about the subject and the point of comparison:

- _____
- _____
- _____

(Continue until you have outlined or sketched a plan for all your body paragraphs.)

Drafting a Conclusion

Your conclusion should reinforce the idea that you have an important reason for comparing the two subjects and leave readers with a comment on the comparison.

- The takeaway for readers about this comparison should be that
_____.

- A reason that I chose to compare and contrast these two subjects is
_____.

Try it yourself!
Draft a conclusion that clarifies the importance of your comparison.

_____
_____
_____

Creating an Intriguing Title

Your title should indicate your topic and say something about it that will interest readers. Try the following ideas to create an intriguing title that your audience will want to read:

- Alliteration: I can use these words that start with the same sound to refer to the subjects I am comparing or to the idea I am conveying about them: _____.

- Groups of three: Three things I talk about in the essay are _____, _____, and _____
_____.

- Question: People ask _____
_____ about the subjects of my comparison-and-contrast essay.

- Quotation: Someone said "_____
_____" about the subjects of my comparison-and-contrast essay.

- Try out a title of your own: _____

FEEDBACK ACTIVITIES

Getting Your Questions Answered by Peer Reviewers

You'll get better feedback from peer reviewers if you ask for specific help with comments and questions like these.

- I'm not sure whether or not _____ is working.
- Does the description of _____ make sense?
- My biggest concern is _____.

Now write the question with which you *most* want your peer reviewers' help:

_____
_____

Asking Reviewers for Feedback about a Comparison-and-Contrast Essay

To find out if reviewers are getting the information they need from your comparison-and-contrast essay, have them answer the following questions.

- What is the thesis? How well does it explain the value of reading this essay?
- Are the subjects similar enough and different enough to make a valuable comparison? Why or why not?
- How well does the organization work to convey the aspects of the subjects that I am comparing and contrasting?
- How well do you understand the similarities and differences between the subjects? What, if anything, is unclear?
- What important questions do you have that are not answered by the essay?
- What details work best for this essay? What do you like about them?
- Which details are weakest? Which ideas need further development?
- How well does the essay hang together? How effective are the transitions between paragraphs?
- How enticing is the introduction? Which parts make you want to keep reading? What is less interesting?
- How well does the conclusion end the essay? What works best to bring the essay to an end? What should change?
- How effective is the title? Why?
- My favorite part of this essay is _____
  _____
  because _____.
- The part that I think needs the most improvement is _____
  _____
  because _____.

Conducting a Self-Review

Put your draft aside for at least one day. Then, read it again, doing your best to pretend that you have never seen it before. Use the Rubric for Assessing Comparison-and-Contrast Essays to rate your draft in its current form. (Your instructor may use other criteria for assessing student writing, so be sure to check with him or her about expectations.)

Rubric for Assessing Comparison-and-Contrast Essays

	Exceeds expectations	Meets expectations	Needs improvement	Does not meet expectations
Focus, purpose, and audience	The essay identifies at least two subjects of comparison, establishes a basis of comparison, and identifies specific points of comparison common to each subject; the topic is fresh and unexpected. The essay's purpose determines whether the paper employs comparison, contrast, or both, and the logic behind the choice is clear. The tone reflects the target audience's profile and the introduction forecasts content or conclusions that will engage the reader. A clear thesis statement encompasses the purpose of comparison or contrast and controls all development; body paragraphs are clearly focused by topic sentences addressing points of comparison.	The essay addresses a comparison or contrast topic that is appropriate to the assignment. The introduction identifies subjects and points of comparison, generally indicates the writer's purpose, and establishes an appropriate tone, but may not clearly identify a basis of comparison or suggest why the paper's content or conclusions might be important or interesting to the target audience. A thesis statement focuses all or most of the development, but may not include forecasting elements that would help engage and focus the reader's attention. Body paragraphs develop the same points of comparison for each subject of comparison addressed, but topic sentences may not sharply focus the content.	A topic is apparent but may be trite or obvious. The essay identifies two or more subjects of comparison but does not establish a basis of comparison or identify points of comparison, or it may fail in some other way to satisfy the assignment's requirements. If a thesis is present, it is not clearly comparative, or is too broad to clarify the purpose or focus the reader's attention. The tone does not match the purpose or is not appropriate for the target audience. Body paragraphs may be too short or too long, and their development is not effectively focused by topic sentences addressing points of comparison. The paper may drift off topic in some passages and shift from comparison to contrast, or some other irrelevant content may be included.	No comparative topic is evident in the introduction, although one subject may be addressed in the first paragraph and another identified without prior indication elsewhere in the paper, or the composition may fail to be comparative in nature by addressing different features or characteristics for each subject (strengths and weaknesses, for example). Impressions and vague abstract statements may generally relate to an identified topic but do not constitute comparison. Body paragraphs are underdeveloped or are undifferentiated, with the paper taking the form of one long paragraph. Irrelevant material may intrude or contradictory material may confuse the reader about the paper's focus or purpose.

	Exceeds expectations	**Meets expectations**	**Needs improvement**	**Does not meet expectations**
Development	The paper provides comprehensive development for each point of comparison or contrast and clearly interprets the significance of the content with respect to the identified purpose. Instructive clarifying detail or description develops each body paragraph, anticipating the readers' questions. Where appropriate, supplementary methods of development are employed to clarify or enrich the reader's understanding of the subjects.	Details serve to effectively engage the audience and support the paper's thesis and topic sentences. The development is sufficient to explain how the subjects are similar or different with respect to each point of comparison, and why their similarity or difference is relevant to the paper's purpose. All content is directly relevant to the thesis, and the development of each body paragraph directly relates to its topic sentence, with no disruption of essay or paragraph unity.	Development lacks specific detail and general statements or claims concerning the subjects, and points of comparison are unsubstantiated or unsupported. The paper fails to clearly explain how the subjects of comparison are similar or different with respect to the points of comparison, so the comparative purpose is not fully achieved. Irrelevant observations or opinions may intrude and distract the reader or obscure the point.	If subjects of comparison are identified, few or no details are included to develop them. General statements are vague or they distort or confuse the thesis, if one is present, rather than serving to validate or clarify it. If two subjects of comparison are addressed, the paper does not clarify the ways in which they are similar or different, so fails to achieve the comparative purpose. Body paragraphs are not unified, being largely constituted of impressions or statements of opinion.
Organization and coherence	Subject-by-subject or point-by-point organization governs consistently throughout. If both comparison and contrast are included, passages are clearly distinguished. Shifts from one subject or point to the next are marked with well-chosen transitional devices.	Development is reasonably organized throughout, using either subject-by-subject or point-by-point organization, but comparison-and-contrast elements may be mixed without clear transition. Transitions from one subject or one point to the next	Organization is attempted but inconsistent, alternating between point by point and subject by subject. Individual sentences are comprehensible, but the reasons governing their sequencing is unclear. Transitions are used improperly, randomly, or repetitively.	The essay has no discernible organization at essay or paragraph level. Disjointed sentences fail to reflect systematic development of either the subjects or points of comparison. No explanatory content is introduced, and the essay

	Exceeds expectations	**Meets expectations**	**Needs improvement**	**Does not meet expectations**
Organization and coherence	Forecasting elements in the introduction prepare the reader for shifts or for the inclusion of passages developed around other methods of development, also effectively organized, so the essay is coherent at essay and paragraph levels.	are appropriately signaled; transitions are adequate but may be used repetitively. Focusing statements in the introduction and conclusion help provide context. The essay is generally coherent throughout.	The introduction and conclusion fail to provide coherence to the progression of body paragraphs. Shifts from one subject or point to the next are not clearly marked. Coherence is generally weak at both essay and paragraph levels.	employs inadequate or misleading transitional devices or organizational cues. Shifts from one subject or point to the next are not signaled. No contextualizing statements are included in either introduction or conclusion; the composition is largely incoherent throughout.
Style and structure	Introductory and body elements establish the subject and points of comparison, engage the audience's favorable attention, and provide a map of the essay's content, arranged in coherent body paragraphs. A conclusion reinforces the purpose and thesis. The essay achieves variety in sentence pattern and type. Tone is skillfully controlled; word choice is apt, varied, and artful.	The introduction identifies subjects and points of comparison, establishes an appropriate tone, and guides the reader into the body of the essay, which is developed in multiple separate paragraphs. A functional conclusion is present. The writing employs little variety of pattern or type, but sentence construction is competent. Diction is generally appropriate to audience and purpose, but phrasing may be repetitive or imprecise.	The essay uses spacing or indention, but paragraphing is weak. Introductory and concluding elements may be underdeveloped or absent entirely. Subjects or points are not distinguished from one another by inclusion in separate, distinct paragraphs. Sentences employ faulty or mixed constructions, with little or no variety in pattern or type. Tone and diction lapse into inappropriate informality or stiffness.	Paragraphing is absent or insufficient to meet the demands of the writing situation, with no distinct introductory or concluding elements included. Body paragraphs are either too short or the body is not organized into separate paragraphs. Sentences are difficult to interpret; the writer does not demonstrate control of grammar or paragraph structure. Tone and diction are contradictory or inappropriate.

	Exceeds expectations	**Meets expectations**	**Needs improvement**	**Does not meet expectations**
Precision and editing	The writer reveals mastery of all elements of grammar, usage, and mechanical conventions. Verb tenses are consistent, with appropriate shifts in passages of transition and forecasting. Uses of second person perspective and passive voice are absent or appropriate. The paper is properly formatted and attractive in appearance and contains few or no editing errors. Overall, the composition is memorable and exemplary.	The essay is largely free of errors in grammar, punctuation, and use of mechanical conventions, though occasional lapses occur. Inappropriate shifts may occasionally be included, but do not create confusion. Passages are punctuated competently, with only minor and infrequent error. The paper is neat, legible, and clear, with formatting of manuscript conventions applied consistently. The paper satisfies the assignment with only scattered editing errors.	The essay is weakened with frequent errors in grammar, punctuation, and the use of mechanical conventions. Parallelism is faulty, and inappropriate shifts are pervasive and distracting. The submission may be crumpled, stained, or torn. Errors in manuscript formatting conventions draw unfavorable attention. Numerous editing errors distract the reader, though perhaps cause little or no confusion.	Verb and pronoun usage, sentence constructions, and diction are consistently faulty. Sentence structure is dysfunctional. Punctuation does not follow conventions. Unedited or illegible writing is confusing. Stains, rips, blots, or printing errors distract the reader and may make parts of the paper illegible. The writer fails to observe manuscript conventions or to satisfy other demands of the assignment. Errors throughout are serious enough to cause confusion and misunderstanding.

Gathering Responses and Collecting Your Thoughts

Gather all the reviewer responses. Make notes about what your reviewers agree and disagree on, moving from most important issues, such as thesis, organization, completeness of the comparisons and contrasts, interest, and support for ideas, to least important, such as spelling and comma placement. List areas where you agree that improvement is needed, and make a plan about what you need to revise. Think about areas of disagreement, too. You make the final decisions about what changes to make, so determine which comments you need to respond to and which you can ignore.

REVISION AND EDITING ACTIVITIES
Identifying Options for Revision Planning

After you have gathered revision comments on your early draft from peer reviewers and your instructor (pp. 159–160), choose one of the following strategies to begin making your revision plan.

- Create a storyboard. On a sticky note or note card, write the main point you are making as you compare and contrast your subjects and put it at the top of your work area. Using separate sticky notes or note cards for each paragraph or example, write down important features such as topic sentences and supporting details. Does your organization make sense? Do the parts work together? Does every paragraph help to support the comparison or contrast? Using sticky notes or note cards of a different color, add notes to each paragraph about how you will strengthen, change, or delete content based on your reviewers' comments and your own. Take photos of the parts of the storyboard so you'll have a record of what you decide, even if you lose your notes.

- Create a graphic organizer. Using either paper and pencil or a digital document, create text boxes representing each introductory paragraph, body paragraph, and conclusion paragraph, and write the main idea of each paragraph in the box. Below it, leave room to revise the main idea. To the right of each main idea box, draw additional boxes for changes, additions, and deletions you have decided to make to supporting details, transitions, and other material in that paragraph.

- Make an annotated outline. Using formal complete sentences or informal phrases, make an outline that shows the current main ideas, supporting details, and the organization of your draft. Using highlighters, colored pens, different colors of type, or some other method to make your changes clearly visible, annotate your outline to show the changes you plan to make to your thesis, dominant impression, organization, supporting ideas, introduction, conclusion, and so on.

- Make a plan of your own. _____
_____
_____
_____

Revising a Comparison-and-Contrast Essay

Following the plan you've created, write a complete revised draft. Repeat as needed until you feel that you have a solid draft that is nearly final.

Using Your Common Issues to Focus Editing of Your Comparison-and-Contrast Essay

Edit for grammar, punctuation, and other common problems you have.

- The two kinds of problems that teachers or peer reviewers point out most often in my writing are _____ and _____.

- I know I sometimes struggle with _____.

Review the information in Part 3 (pp. 205–42) about the errors you have identified above. Then reread your draft again, correcting any such errors and any other issues that you find.

Proofreading

- Run the spell-checker and carefully consider every suggestion. Do not automatically accept the suggestions! Remember that spell-checkers cannot identify problems with certain kinds of words, such as homonyms and proper nouns (names), so check the spelling of such words yourself. If you keep track of the words you commonly misspell, you can improve your spelling, so consider a spelling-mistake list based on what you find.

- Read your essay aloud slowly, noting and correcting any issues that you find.

- Read your essay aloud backward, word by word, looking for repeated words and similar mistakes that are easy to miss in work that is very familiar. Correct any problems you see.

When your work is as error-free and professional as you can make it, submit your essay.

12

CAUSE AND EFFECT

PREWRITING ACTIVITIES

Finding Ideas for a Cause-and-Effect Essay Topic

A cause-and-effect essay analyzes the causes that bring about one or more effects, traces an effect back to one or more causes, or both. To identify causes or effects that can serve as the starting point for your cause-and-effect essay, try the following prompts.

- I am lucky that _____ happened so that I _____.
- If _____ is not stopped, the terrible results could include _____ or even _____.
- We wanted to find out why _____ happened and ensure that it would be [more likely/less likely] to happen again.
- Surprisingly, an important reason for _____ is _____.

Try it yourself!
Identify one or more causes for which you will identify effects or work backward from one or more effects to identify causes.

_____
_____
_____
_____

Clustering to Find Ideas for a Cause-and-Effect Essay Topic

To generate ideas for the topic of a cause-and-effect essay, try clustering. Write an idea, either for an event that you see as causing effects or for a result for which you will identify causes, in the middle of a sheet of paper and circle it. Then, write causes or effects of the central idea around it, circling each and joining it to the central circle. If you are certain that there is a causal connection, use a solid line to connect the circles, but use a dotted line if you need to find out more about whether the events are linked. Keep going, generating ideas related to circled concepts as you think of them, until the paper is filled. (You can also use software for digital clustering diagrams if you prefer.)

- What ideas were most productive for you, prompting the largest clusters of circled words and phrases?
- Which connections are most surprising? Will any require evidence?
- Are any ideas unexpectedly unproductive, going nowhere on your diagram? Pay attention to what doesn't work as well as to what does.
- What connections seem most likely to interest you and your readers?

Identifying a Preliminary Topic for a Cause-and-Effect Essay

What causal relationship will you talk about in your essay? The topic can be one that you started with on this page, or it can be an idea that came to you while you were exploring something else in one of the previous activities.

- My preliminary topic is _____

_____
_____.

Finding a Perspective on the Preliminary Topic for Your Cause-and-Effect Essay

In order to find examples that will work well for your cause-and-effect essay, you should consider your point of view of the topic.

- This topic makes me feel _____
  _____.

- I want anyone who reads my cause-and-effect essay to know that
  _____
  _____.

- The best way to show my point of view is to include _____,
  _____, and _____.

Identifying the Readers for Your Cause-and-Effect Essay

Figuring out what your audience already knows and does not know about the topic will be extremely important. If you consider what they already believe or know, you will be able to determine what you need to prove and what kinds of evidence will be most convincing. Complete the following prompts to analyze the audience you expect to reach.

- My audience includes _____.
- They may already know _____
  about this topic, but they may not know _____
  _____.

- I need to tell this audience about _____
  _____ so they will
  understand my perspective on the topic.

- When they read my essay, I want them to feel _____
  _____

- My purpose for writing is to _____.

Exploring Logical Ideas for a Cause-and-Effect Essay

What are some logical, persuasive, and interesting points you will need to make to clarify the chain of causes and effects? Respond to any of the following prompts that are appropriate for your cause-and-effect essay.

- A cause that everyone associates with this effect is _____. It is [useful/not useful] for my cause-and-effect essay because _____.

- An effect that people assume comes from this cause is _____. It is [useful/not useful] for my cause-and-effect essay because _____.

- A visual that would clarify the causes and effects is _____.

- My own experience with _____ could be used as [a cause/an effect] in the causal chain I am writing about because _____.

- I [need/do not need] to use sources from research.
- Additional sources I could use include _____, and I can find them _____.

Identifying Strong, Vivid Examples for a Cause-and-Effect Essay

Sensory details can make a cause-and-effect essay come alive. Brainstorm as many of the following prompts as possible to try out different details to enliven the information you will include.

- something seen, observed, or watched that is part of a causal connection

    EXAMPLES: fewer songbirds at my backyard feeder since the neighbors began letting their cat go outside

    _____

- a sound that relates to causes or effects

    EXAMPLES: the wall of sound rumbling from the stack of Marshall amplifiers that stood behind the guitarist, who now has difficulty hearing certain frequencies

    _____

- an aroma, smell, or stench that is relevant to the causal connection

    EXAMPLES: the smell of cinnamon that contributed to the nausea I felt while waiting for my flight to depart

    _____

    _____

    _____

- something tangible or textured that relates to a cause or an effect

    EXAMPLES: the solid thunk of the bag connecting with the heel of my hand as I dove into second base

    _____

    _____

    _____

- a flavor or taste that connects to a cause or an effect

    EXAMPLES: the creamy taste of the high-fat chocolate ice cream I enjoyed every day that summer before I found that my back-to-school wardrobe was too small

    _____

    _____

    _____

- Try creating an example from any method of development that seems useful.

    _____

    _____

    _____

Choosing Visuals or Other Media to Enliven a Cause-and-Effect Essay

If you have access to photos or other media that will help create a vivid impression of one or more of the causes or effects you are discussing, consider including one or more of them in your essay. Video and audio files can be used in an essay that you will post online.

THESIS ACTIVITIES

- My preliminary topic (p. 168) is _____.

Narrowing and Focusing a Topic for a Cause-and-Effect Essay

Will you be able to clarify all of the causes and effects you will need to make your case in an essay of the assigned length? Sometimes a narrower topic may allow you to create a better cause-and-effect essay.

- If I had five minutes to explain the most important cause-and-effect relationship to people who are not familiar with it, I would start with _____ _____ _____.

Identifying a Main Point for Your Cause-and-Effect Essay

To me, the single most important thing about the topic I am trying to illustrate is (pick one and complete the sentence)

- that it explains _____.
- that it helps people understand _____.
- that it proves _____.
- that it is exciting because _____.
- that it is important because _____.
- that _____ _____.

Moving from Topic to Preliminary Thesis for a Cause-and-Effect Essay

Fill in the blanks to start thinking about the point you want to make in your cause-and-effect essay.

- Many people will be surprised to find out that _____ [causes/affects] _____.

- I used to believe _____ about the cause or effect I am describing, but I have changed my mind. Now I think _____.

- This may sound strange, but [the causal relationship] makes me think about _____ because _____.

- At first I did not understand [the relationship between cause and effect], but now I think of it as _____
  _____.

- A new insight my readers should have about [the causal relationship] is
  _____.

Now, write your statement about the cause-and-effect relationship that can serve as a preliminary thesis.

_____
_____

Testing Your Thesis

In a sentence or two, explain your proposed thesis for your cause-and-effect essay to a classmate or friend who is part of your audience, and briefly tell him or her about how you propose to support the thesis. Ask for responses to these questions.

- How much do you understand about the relationship between the cause(s) and effect(s) I'm describing?
  _____
  _____

- How convincing is my plan to demonstrate the relationship between the cause(s) and effect(s) in my essay? Why? _____
  _____

- What interests you most about this topic? Why? _____
  _____

Do the reviewer's responses suggest that you are on the right track? If not, consider whether you should rethink your topic, review your assumptions about what your audience knows and cares about, or find better evidence to show the relationship between the causes and effects.

DRAFTING ACTIVITIES

Deciding Where to Begin

Begin at the easiest point for you to get started. If starting with the cause will help you get your draft underway, begin there; if the effect is more interesting or easier to write about, begin with that. You may want to begin with ideas you know your readers will accept and then turn later to proving less clear connections. You can start with the introduction, of course, but you do not have to begin at the beginning; you can draft the introduction and conclusion after the body of your essay if that will help you get started.

Brainstorming Ways to Get Readers' Attention

Keeping your preliminary thesis in mind, try your hand at these effective ways to start an introduction.

- a quotation (something you said, something someone said to you, a relevant snippet of dialogue that will be part of one of your examples)

- an anecdote or story (something that sheds light on the subject you are discussing or explains how you came to realize the connection between causes and effects)

- a provocative statement (a surprising or shocking announcement or an unexpected revelation)

- a question that prompts readers to think about how they will answer it

- a hypothetical situation that invites others to imagine being in someone else's place

- a comparison that shows how your unfamiliar concept is like something more familiar to your readers

Drafting an Introduction

Choose the opening you like most from the examples you've created, and start a new draft that begins with that opening. How can you move from this catchy opening to your first example?

- State the cause-and-effect relationship clearly rather than asking readers to guess.
- What background information will readers need right up front to make sense of your thesis? How can you incorporate it smoothly?
- How will you help readers get a sense of the scope of the information you will provide? How can you make yourself seem trustworthy?

Trying Options for Organizing Body Paragraphs

If you aren't certain what organization makes sense for the examples that will support your thesis, try completing any of the following options that seems viable. Use the option you choose as the basis for an outline or graphic organizer that you can follow as you draft.

By Time

- Chronological order: start with the earliest cause(s) and move forward in time to the most recent effect(s)
- Reverse chronological order: start with most recent effect(s) and move backward to the earliest cause(s)

Point by Point or Subject by Subject (for Multiple Causes and Effects)

- Start with the first cause and first effect, then give the second cause and second effect, then the third cause and third effect, and so on
- Present the first cause, second cause, and third cause together; then present the first effect, second effect, third effect, and so on

As a Causal Chain

- Start with the first cause and effect; then use the first effect as the second cause that leads to a new effect; then use the second effect as a third cause, and so on.

Try it yourself!

- Organization plan for examples: _____

Topic of first body paragraph: _____

- Causes and/or effects to discuss: _____

    Details and evidence to include in the paragraph:

    - _____
    - _____
    - _____

Topic of second body paragraph: _____

- Causes and/or effects to discuss: _____

    Details and evidence to include in the paragraph:

    - _____
    - _____
    - _____

Topic of third body paragraph: _____

- Causes and/or effects to discuss: _____

    Details and evidence to include in the paragraph:

    - _____
    - _____
    - _____

(Continue until you have outlined or sketched a plan for all your body paragraphs.)

Drafting a Conclusion

Your conclusion should reinforce the point you are making by presenting the causes and effects you have discussed. It should also make a memorable final statement.

- The point of this cause-and-effect analysis is _____
  _____.

- Thinking about these causes and effects is important because _____
  _____.

- Readers should feel _____.

Try it yourself!
Draft a conclusion that reinforces your thesis and ties the whole essay together:

_____

_____

_____

Creating an Intriguing Title

Your title should indicate the topic of your cause-and-effect essay and say something about it that will interest readers. Try the following ideas to create an intriguing title that your audience will want to read.

- Alliteration: My causes and effects relate mainly to _____ _____, and some words that begin with the same sound and relate to my examples are _____ _____.

- Groups of three: Three things that are important to the cause-and-effect relationship I'm discussing are _____, _____, and _____.

- Question: People wonder _____ _____ about this cause-and-effect relationship.

- Quotation: Someone said "_____ _____" about this causal relationship.

- Try out a title of your own: _____.

FEEDBACK ACTIVITIES

Getting Your Questions Answered by Peer Reviewers

You'll get better feedback from peer reviewers if you ask for specific help with comments and questions like these.

- I'm not sure whether or not _____ is working.

- Is the evidence for a cause-and-effect relationship between _____ _____ and _____ convincing?
- My biggest concern is _____.

Now write the question with which you *most* want your peer reviewers' help.

_____

_____

Asking Reviewers for Feedback about a Cause-and-Effect Essay

To find out if reviewers are getting the impression you want to give in your cause-and-effect essay, have them answer the following questions.

- What is the thesis? Is it interesting?
- How persuasively does the essay explain the relationship between the causes and the effects? What evidence is most and least convincing?
- What questions are not answered that should be answered?
- What details work well? What do you like about them?
- Which details are weakest? Which ideas need further development?
- Does the essay's organization make sense?
- How well does the essay hang together? How effective are the transitions between paragraphs?
- How enticing is the introduction? Which parts make you want to keep reading? What is less interesting?
- How well does the conclusion end the essay? What works best to bring the essay to an end? What should change?
- How effective is the title? Why?
- My favorite part of this essay is _____

  because _____.
- The part that I think needs the most improvement is _____

  because _____.

Conducting a Self-Review

Put your draft aside for at least one day. Then, read it again, doing your best to pretend that you have never seen it before. Use the Rubric for Assessing Cause-and-Effect Essays to see how well you think you have accomplished the essay's objectives in this draft. (Your instructor may use other criteria for assessing student writing, so be sure to check with him or her about expectations.)

Rubric for Assessing Cause-and-Effect Essays

	Exceeds expectations	Meets expectations	Needs improvement	Does not meet expectations
Focus, purpose, and audience	The thesis addresses a term or concept that is interesting and important to the audience. The introduction indicates how the essay will clarify, explain, or support the thesis by using cause and effect and promises an insight or learning experience. Unified body paragraphs have clearly focused topic sentences.	The thesis addresses a claim, term, or concept appropriate to the audience and the assignment. The introduction clearly indicates the intent to clarify or support the thesis by using cause and effect. Unified body paragraphs include functional topic sentences.	A thesis is evident but is too broad or narrow or does not meet the assignment's purpose or appeal to the target audience. Body paragraphs are too broadly or too narrowly focused or lack clearly governing topic sentences. Some irrelevant material may be included.	No clear thesis is evident, or the thesis is inadequate to control the essay or engage the reader's favorable attention. Body paragraphs lack topic sentences or are too long or too short to effectively develop individual subtopics.
Development	The essay offers well-chosen, authoritative, representative, relevant, and concrete examples to clarify and support the paper's thesis and engage the	Examples are appropriate to the audience and purpose and sufficient to adequately support the thesis, but may be left to "speak for themselves" without being	Examples are offered to support the thesis, but are too broad or too general to fully engage the audience or validate the thesis. Development may be overbalanced	Few examples are offered or they distort or confuse the thesis rather than serving to validate or clarify it.

	Exceeds expectations	Meets expectations	Needs improvement	Does not meet expectations
Development	audience's favorable attention. Extended examples are fully integrated with the explanatory content; personal experience examples are balanced with historical, topical, or other examples that can be authenticated.	fully integrated with the paper or paragraph topic. Essay and paragraph content is relevant, with no disruption of essay or paragraph unity and no visible bias.	with unverifiable personal experience or hypothetical examples.	
Organization and coherence	Clear, logical organizing principles govern the arrangement of content at both essay and paragraph levels. Forecasting statements are used effectively in the introduction. Smooth, largely unnoticed transitions within and between ideas and paragraphs enhance coherence.	Development is reasonably organized throughout. Sentences within paragraphs are arranged to show the logical sequencing of ideas. Each body paragraph is unified and coherent. Body paragraphs are sequenced effectively for the type(s) of examples employed. Transitions link ideas and paragraphs.	Organization is attempted but is ineffective or unclear. The reader can follow the writer's points with difficulty. Body paragraph sequencing seems uncontrolled or random, with insufficient or confusing transitional, organizational cues being employed.	The essay has no discernible organization at the essay or paragraph level. The reader is unable to follow the writer's train of thought, and the essay employs inadequate or misleading transitional devices or organizational cues.

Feedback Activities

	Exceeds expectations	Meets expectations	Needs improvement	Does not meet expectations
Style and structure	Design of introductory, body, and concluding elements engages the audience's favorable attention and guides them through the essay's content, arranged in coherent body paragraphs. A conclusion prompts rethinking of the topic or promotes new insight. The essay achieves variety in sentence pattern and type. If using sources, the writer uses signal phrasing and clearly sets off cited from original material. Tone is skillfully controlled; word choice is apt.	The introduction addresses the topic, sets the tone, and guides the reader into the body of the paper, which is developed in multiple separate paragraphs. A functional conclusion is present. The writing employs little variety, but sentence construction is competent. If used, sources are acknowledged, but signal phrasing or parenthetical elements may be misplaced or confusing. Diction is appropriate, but may be repetitive or imprecise.	The essay uses spacing or indention, but paragraphing is weak. Introductory elements are not controlled, and a separate body and conclusion may not be included. Sentences are vague or ambiguous, with little or no variety in pattern or type. If outside sources are used, no in-text citation is offered, or it is too confusing to clearly distinguish the writer's work from cited material. Tone is inappropriate for the purpose and audience. Diction is faulty or inappropriate.	Paragraphing is absent or insufficient to meet the demands of the writing situation, with no distinct introductory or concluding elements included. Sentences are difficult to interpret; the writer does not demonstrate control of grammar or paragraph structure. Tone and diction are confusing, contradictory, or inappropriate.
Precision and editing	The writer reveals mastery of all elements of grammar, usage, and mechanical conventions. Listed examples are punctuated properly and are parallel in	The essay is largely free of errors in grammar, punctuation, and use of mechanical conventions, though occasional lapses occur. Sentences are coherent, and	The essay has frequent errors in grammar, punctuation, and the use of mechanical conventions. Where outside sources are used, the bibliographic	Verb and pronoun usage, sentence constructions, and diction are consistently faulty. Sentence structure is dysfunctional. Punctuation is arbitrary.

	Exceeds expectations	Meets expectations	Needs improvement	Does not meet expectations
Precision and editing	construction. Where outside sources are used, they are cited in proper bibliographic form. Formatting conventions for use of font and line spacing, use of headings, headers and footers are applied appropriately throughout. An attractive page design draws the reader's eye through the page. The writer executes the assignment memorably with no careless errors.	structural errors (where present) do not disrupt the reading. Where outside sources are used, proper bibliographic form and mechanical conventions are employed, with minor lapses in form or format. The paper is neat, legible, and clear, with formatting of manuscript conventions applied consistently. The paper satisfies the assignment with only scattered careless errors.	information is included but is formatted incorrectly, sometimes leading to ambiguity of source or source type. The submission may be crumpled, stained, or torn. Errors in manuscript formatting conventions draw unfavorable attention. The writer attempts but fails to fully execute the assignment. Numerous careless errors distract, though perhaps cause little or no confusion.	Where outside sources are used, bibliographic entries are omitted or incomplete. Careless or illegible writing is confusing. Stains, tears, blots, or printing errors distract the reader and may make parts of the paper unreadable. The writer fails to observe manuscript conventions or to satisfy other demands of the assignment. Errors throughout are serious enough to cause confusion and misunderstanding of meaning.

Gathering Responses and Collecting Your Thoughts

Gather all the reviewer responses. Make notes about what you and your reviewers agree and disagree on, moving from most important issues, such as appropriateness of the topic, the effectiveness of the examples, the organization, and the support for ideas, to least important, such as spelling and comma placement. List areas where you agree that improvement is needed, and make a plan about what you need to revise. Think about areas of disagreement, too. You make the final decisions about what changes to make, so determine which comments you need to respond to and which you can ignore.

REVISION AND EDITING ACTIVITIES

Identifying Options for Revision Planning

After you have gathered revision comments on your early draft from peer reviewers and your instructor (pp. 177–78), choose one of the following strategies to begin making your revision plan.

- Create a storyboard. On a sticky note or note card, write the main point you are making about cause and effect and put it at the top of your work area. Using separate sticky notes or note cards for each paragraph or example, write down important features such as topic sentences and supporting details. Does your organization make sense? Do the parts work together? Does every paragraph help to advance the story and clarify the point it makes? Using sticky notes or note cards of a different color, add notes to each paragraph about how you will strengthen, change, or delete content based on your reviewers' comments and your own. Take photos of the parts of the storyboard so you'll have a record of what you decide, even if you lose your notes.

- Create a graphic organizer. Using either paper and pencil or a digital document, create text boxes representing each introductory paragraph, body paragraph, and conclusion paragraph, and write the main idea of each paragraph in the box. Below it, leave room to revise the main idea. To the right of each main idea box, draw additional boxes for changes, additions, and deletions you have decided to make to supporting details, transitions, and other material in that paragraph.

- Make an annotated outline. Using either formal complete sentences or informal phrases, make an outline that shows the current main ideas, supporting details, and organization of your draft. Using highlighters, colored pens, different colors of type, or some other method to make your changes clearly visible, annotate your outline to show the changes you plan to make to your thesis, dominant impression, organization, supporting ideas, introduction, conclusion, and so on.

- Make a plan of your own. _____
_____
_____
_____

Revising a Cause-and-Effect Essay

Following the plan you've created, write a complete revised draft. Repeat as needed until you feel that you have a solid draft that is nearly final.

Using Your Common Issues to Focus Editing of Your Cause-and-Effect Essay

Edit for grammar, punctuation, and other common problems you have.

- The two kinds of problems that teachers or peer reviewers point out most often in my writing are _____ and _____.
- I know I sometimes struggle with _____.

Review the information in Part 3 (pp. 205–42) about the errors you have identified above. Then reread your draft again, correcting any such errors and other issues that you find.

Proofreading

- Run the spell-checker and carefully consider every suggestion. Do not automatically accept the suggestions! Remember that spell-checkers cannot identify problems with certain kinds of words, such as homonyms and proper nouns (names), so check the spelling of such words yourself. Write the words you have misspelled on a spelling checklist you can use to identify and avoid words that give you trouble.
- Read your essay aloud slowly, noting and correcting any issues that you find.
- Read your essay aloud backward, word by word, looking for repeated words and similar mistakes that are easy to miss in work that is very familiar. Correct any problems you see.

When your work is as error-free and professional as you can make it, submit your essay.

13

ARGUMENT

PREWRITING ACTIVITIES

Finding Issues for an Argument Essay

An argument essay makes a logical, persuasive claim on an issue about which people can reasonably disagree. To identify arguable claims that can serve as the starting point for your argument essay, try the following prompts.

- I recently had a heated discussion with [a friend/an acquaintance/a family member] about _____ because [she/he] believes _____ and I believe _____.

- When I read about _____, it makes me [angry/unhappy/inspired/hopeful].

- People who want _____ should _____ and not _____.

- Individuals can make a difference in my community by _____
  _____,
  but few people are willing to make the effort.

- _____ is a problem
  because _____,
  and one way to make it better is _____.

Try it yourself!

Identify one or more topics you might be interested in tackling in an argument essay.

_____

_____

_____

Freewriting to Find Arguable Issues for an Argument Essay

To generate ideas for an argument essay, try starting with freewriting to discover what you know, what you need to find out, and how you feel about an issue. Set a timer for five minutes and write without stopping, putting down every thought about your argument that comes to mind. If a new thought derails your initial idea, can you find ways to use that idea persuasively? Keep going, generating as many ideas and comments as you can, until the time is up.

- Read over what you wrote, and highlight or underline words, phrases, and sentences that strike you as interesting or useful in some way.

- In a new document, write (or copy and paste) the most interesting words or phrases you called out from the first round of freewriting. Set the timer for another five minutes and use your initial freewriting prompts to generate more ideas.

- Keep going until you have some ideas to get started on your argument essay.

Identifying a Tentative Claim for an Argument Essay

What issue will you talk about in your essay, and what position do you intend to argue? The topic can be one that you started with on this page, or it can be an idea that came to you while you were exploring something else in one of the activities above.

- My tentative claim is _____
  _____
  _____.

Collaborating to Identify Opposing Arguments

Now that you have a tentative claim for a topic for your argument essay, make sure that it is arguable. Jot down as much supporting evidence as you can for the topic, and then write down all the opposing evidence you can think of. Working with a partner, take turns reading your points, both pro and con, and asking the partner to identify any weaknesses in either the supporting or the opposing argument and to identify the strongest and most persuasive points on both sides of the issue. Take notes of points your partner brings up so you can determine how to address them.

Finding a Perspective on the Preliminary Topic for Your Argument Essay

In order to find examples that will work well for your argument essay, you should consider your point of view of the topic.

- My perspective on this topic is _____
  _____.

- I want anyone who reads my argument essay to know that _____
  _____.

- The best way to show my point of view is to include _____,
  _____, and _____.

Identifying the Readers for Your Argument Essay

Figuring out what your audience already knows and does not know about the topic will be extremely important. If you consider what they already believe or know, you will be able to determine what you need to prove and what kinds of evidence will be most convincing. Complete the following prompts to analyze the audience you expect to reach.

- My audience includes _____.
- Some of them probably agree with me about _____.
- I may convince those who do not agree with my perspective on the topic to take my argument seriously if _____.

- The kind of evidence that this audience will find convincing is most likely _____.

- I need to tell this audience about _____ _____ so they will understand my perspective on the topic.

- When they read my argument essay, I want them to feel _____ _____.

- When they read my argument essay, I would ideally like them to do ____ _____.

- My purpose for writing is to _____.

Exploring the Library to Find Logical and Persuasive Evidence for an Argument

To find the most persuasive evidence to support your ideas and refute opposing ideas for an argument, you will probably need to do library research. A preliminary visit to the library to look for books and articles is a good place to begin. List your responses to the prompts below and then talk with reference librarians about how to find useful sources; a librarian's advice will probably save you time and produce better results.

- Types of evidence that may change the minds of people who don't agree with me yet: _____ _____

- Types of evidence I need to find to prove what I already believe to be true: _____ _____

- Other information I need to make my case: _____ _____

- Possible sources for the most persuasive opposing viewpoints that I will need to address: _____ _____ _____

Collaborating to Explore Opposing Viewpoints

After doing library research and talking with a partner about the pros and cons of the issue, you should have a sense of the most important opposing arguments that your argument essay will need to address. Jot down information about each opposing argument (and the source, if you are quoting or paraphrasing someone else's words) on a note card. Working with a group of classmates, read the information, and then discuss with the group whether the argument has any of the following issues.

- Credibility: Is the source an expert? Is there evidence that the source is biased? Are there other reasons to question the accuracy of the argument?

- Relevance here and now: When was the argument made—recently or long ago? Has anything changed significantly since then? Is the argument still valid? Does the argument address the same situation in the same place that you are talking about?

- Counterexamples: Can you identify examples, anecdotes, or stories to refute the points in the argument?

Identifying Good Reasons for Your Argument

After you've looked at ways to argue against opposing claims, brainstorm reasons in support of the tentative claim you are making. (For help making claims based on sources, see Chapter 14, "Sentence Guides for Academic Writers," on pp. 207–17.)

- Experts say _____
  _____
  _____.

- My experience shows _____
  _____
  _____.

- Facts and statistics demonstrate _____
  _____
  _____.

- A convincing visual that would support my point is _____
  _____
  _____.

THESIS ACTIVITIES

- My tentative claim (p. 187) is _____.

Narrowing and Focusing a Topic for an Argument Essay

Will you be able to argue this claim effectively in an essay of the assigned length? Sometimes a narrower topic may allow you to create a better argument essay.

- If I had five minutes to explain the essence of my argument to people who are not familiar with it, I would start with _____
_____
_____.

Identifying a Main Point for Your Argument Essay

To me, the single most important thing about my tentative claim is (pick one and complete the sentence)

- that it would help _____.
- that it would improve understanding of _____.
- that it could prove _____.
- that _____
_____.

Moving from Tentative Claim to Preliminary Thesis for an Argument Essay

If you still need to strengthen your tentative claim, fill in the blanks to start thinking about the point you want to make in your argument essay.

- Many people will be surprised to find out that _____
_____.

- I used to believe _____, but I have changed my mind. Now I think _____
_____.

- At first I did not understand _____
but now _____.

- A new insight I want my readers to gain from reading my essay is _____
_____.

Now, write your statement about the argument relationship that can serve as a preliminary thesis.

_____

_____

_____

Testing Your Thesis

In a sentence or two, explain your proposed thesis for your argument essay to a classmate or friend who is part of your audience, and briefly tell him or her about how you propose to support the thesis. Ask for responses to these questions.

- Does the thesis make a claim that a reasonable person could disagree with?

  _____

  _____

- How easily could this claim be refuted? Is it too absolute? _____

  _____

- What interests you most about this topic? Why? _____

  _____

Do the reviewers' responses suggest that you are on the right track? If not, consider whether you should rethink your thesis, review your assumptions about what your audience knows and cares about, or find better evidence to support your claim.

DRAFTING ACTIVITIES

Deciding Where to Begin

Begin at the easiest point for you to get started. If starting with an opposing argument will help you get underway, start there; if you want to begin by making your own case, do so. You can start with the introduction, of course, but you do not have to begin at the beginning; you can draft the introduction and conclusion after you have completed the body of your essay if that will help you get started.

Brainstorming Ways to Get Readers' Attention

Keeping your preliminary thesis in mind, try your hand at these effective ways to start an introduction.

- a quotation (something you said, something someone said to you, a relevant snippet of dialogue that will be part of one of your examples)

  _____
  _____

- an anecdote or story (something that sheds light on the subject you are discussing or explains how you came to realize the connection between causes and effects)

  _____
  _____

- a provocative piece of information (a surprising or shocking fact from your research or an unexpected revelation)

  _____
  _____

- a question that prompts readers to think about how they will answer it

  _____
  _____

- a hypothetical situation that invites others to imagine being in someone else's place

  _____
  _____

- a comparison that shows how your unfamiliar concept is like something more familiar to your readers

  _____
  _____

Drafting an Introduction

Choose the opening you like most from the examples you've created, and start a new draft that begins with that opening. How can you move from this catchy opening to your thesis? Complete the relevant prompts to brainstorm ways to provide everything your readers need from you.

- I should present the issue by _____
  _____.

- Background information my readers may not know includes _____
  _____.

- Terms I may need to define include _____
  _____.
- To make readers feel that I am trustworthy and likable, I will _____
  _____.

Trying Options for Organizing Body Paragraphs

If you aren't certain what organization makes sense for the evidence that will support your thesis, try different options. You can begin with strongest claims or build up from weaker claims to stronger ones, or you may move from more to less familiar or less to more familiar claims.

Deductive Methods

- Present your claim, then the reasons and evidence, and then present and refute opposing views.
- Present your claim, then present and refute opposing views, and finally, present your reasons and evidence.

Inductive Methods

- Present your reasons and evidence, then present and refute opposing views, and finally, present your claim.
- Present opposing views, present your reasons and evidence, and finally, present your claim.

Try it yourself!

- Use graphic organizers or outlines to try different possibilities.

Topic of first body paragraph: _____.

Information and evidence to include in the paragraph:

- _____
- _____
- _____

Topic of second body paragraph: _____.

Information and evidence to include in the paragraph:

- _____
- _____
- _____

Topic of third body paragraph: _____.

Information and evidence to include in the paragraph:

- _____
- _____
- _____

(Continue until you have outlined or sketched a plan for all your body paragraphs.)

Drafting a Conclusion

Your conclusion should reinforce the point you are making in your thesis. It should also make a memorable final statement, appeal to readers' values, and perhaps ask them to take action.

- The takeaway from my argument essay should be _____
  _____.

- Readers should feel _____
  and do _____.

Try it yourself!
Draft a conclusion that reinforces your thesis and ties the whole essay together.

_____
_____
_____

Creating an Intriguing Title

Your title should indicate the topic of your argument essay and say something about it that will interest readers. Try the following ideas to create an intriguing title that your audience will want to read.

- Alliteration: My issue relates mainly to _____
  _____ and some words that begin with the same sound and relate to my argument are _____
  _____.

- Groups of three: Three things that are important to the argument I'm making are _____, _____
  _____, and _____.

- Question: People wonder _____

  about this argument.
- Quotation: Someone said "_____
  _____" about this argument.
- Try out a title of your own: _____

FEEDBACK ACTIVITIES

Getting Your Questions Answered by Peer Reviewers

You'll get better feedback from peer reviewers if you ask for specific help with comments and questions like these.

- I'm not sure whether or not _____ is working.
- Is the evidence for my claim convincing? Why or why not?
- My biggest concern is _____.

Now write the question with which you *most* want your peer reviewers' help.

_____

_____

_____

Asking Reviewers for Feedback about an Argument Essay

To find out if reviewers are getting the impressions you want to give in your argument essay, have them answer the following questions.

- What is the thesis? Is it interesting?
- How persuasively does the essay make its case? What evidence is most and least convincing?
- What questions are not answered that should be answered?
- What sources are most useful (if the essay includes research)? How effectively are they included? Does the essay include a works-cited page or list of references?
- What details work well? What do you like about them?
- Which details are weakest? Which ideas need further development?

- Does the essay's organization make sense?
- How well does the essay hang together? How effective are the transitions between paragraphs?
- How enticing is the introduction? Which parts make you want to keep reading? What is less interesting?
- How well does the conclusion end the essay? What works best to bring the essay to an end? What should change?
- How effective is the title? Why?
- My favorite part of this essay is _____ because _____.
- The part that I think needs the most improvement is _____ because _____.

Conducting a Self-Review

Put your draft aside for at least one day. Then, read it again, doing your best to pretend that you have never seen it before. Use the Rubric for Assessing Argument Essays to see how well you think you have accomplished the essay's objectives in this draft. (Your instructor may use other criteria for assessing student writing, so be sure to check with him or her about expectations.)

Rubric for Assessing Argument Essays

Exceeds expectations	Meets expectations	Needs improvement	Does not meet expectations
The thesis challenges an open-minded but skeptical audience by addressing an important, current subject of public debate or controversy. The	The thesis addresses an academic audience on a topic of public discussion, but the topic may be too overworked to effectively engage the	A thesis is evident but may be more analytical than persuasive, failing to address a subject with multiple valid perspectives, or it may not clearly	No clear thesis is evident, or the thesis is inadequate to control the essay or engage the reader's favorable attention. The introduction, if present, fails to

	Exceeds expectations	Meets expectations	Needs improvement	Does not meet expectations
Focus, purpose, and audience	introduction engages the audience's favorable attention, briefly addresses the key perspectives, defines relevant terms, identifies shared values, or uses Rogerian strategy to minimize tension and establish goodwill. The essay indicates what the writer wants the audience to think, believe, or do after reading the paper, and this purpose is appropriate given the target audience. Body paragraphs focus individually on each key point or reason for each perspective, effectively supporting one position and refuting the other(s).	readers' favorable attention. The introduction briefly addresses the key perspectives, defines relevant terms, and attempts to establish goodwill, but may not fully alleviate tension generated by conflicting viewpoints. The paper generally suggests what the writer wants to achieve—what he or she wants the audience to think, believe, or do after reading—but this purpose may be unrealistic, given the target audience. Body paragraphs focus on key points informing each perspective, supporting one position and attempting to refute the other(s).	meet the assignment's persuasive requirement, identify the purpose it will attempt to serve, or appeal to an academic audience. The introduction fails to address multiple perspectives and is ineffective in attempts to establish goodwill or convince the reader to continue reading. Body paragraphs are too broadly or too narrowly focused or lack clearly governing topic sentences. The paper does not develop arguments for both perspectives or fails to adequately support one and refute the other. Some irrelevant material may be included.	address a subject of argument appropriate to the assignment or indicate a purpose. If a subject of debate is identified, the introduction fails to address the perspectives adequately. Content may not be organized into separate body paragraphs. If present, body paragraphs lack topic sentences or are too long or too short to effectively develop individual subtopics. The paper takes no position on the subject of argument or acknowledges only one perspective. Irrelevant or inappropriately subjective personal commentary distorts the focus.

	Exceeds expectations	Meets expectations	Needs improvement	Does not meet expectations
Development	The paper offers an interesting balance of general statement and concrete supporting detail and is ample and authoritative, fully illustrating each point in each perspective's argument. The development in each body paragraph is directly relevant to its topic sentence and is appropriate to the mode of development employed at the paragraph level to develop the points of argument for each perspective and refutation. Counterevidence is acknowledged and addressed without distortion.	Content at the essay level is appropriate to the audience and purpose and sufficient to adequately support the thesis, but may lack specific or explicit detail. Paragraph development is relevant to topic sentences, with no extraneous material to disrupt unity. Both perspectives are developed with relevant evidence taken from valid research. Counterevidence is acknowledged and the writer's argument attempts to accommodate it with little or no evident bias.	Development offered to support the thesis is limited to generalization or is insufficient to fully engage the audience or validate the thesis. Vagueness, inaccuracy, or unclear reasoning may confuse the audience or leave the reader unconvinced of the thesis' validity. Body paragraphs do not clearly correlate to individual points developing each perspective and are not informed by authoritative research. Bias is evident throughout.	Vague claims are unsubstantiated. Reasoning is distorted or unclear. If a thesis is discernible, attempts to develop it are limited to statements of personal opinion or conjecture. Content is not always directly relevant to the essay's subject. Body paragraphs are either too underdeveloped to support each subtopic or are undifferentiated and form one long, unfocused paragraph lacking unity. The paper is too subjective to function as academic writing.
	Clear, logical inductive or deductive organizing principles appropriate to the purpose and audience are	Development is reasonably organized throughout, primarily according to deductive order. Subtopics follow	Organization is attempted but is ineffective or unclear. The reader can follow the writer's points with difficulty. The introduction	The essay has no discernible organization at the essay or paragraph level. The reader is unable to follow the writer's train of

	Exceeds expectations	Meets expectations	Needs improvement	Does not meet expectations
Organization and coherence	employed at both essay and paragraph levels. The introduction offers a brief "essay map" forecasting the sequencing of subtopics. Each body paragraph uses an organizing approach appropriate to its role in developing the argument. Transitions effectively clarify relationships between ideas and subtopics throughout.	a sequence suggested by forecasting elements in the introduction. Each body paragraph uses an organizing approach appropriate to its mode of development. Body paragraphs are sequenced effectively, leading to coherence of the essay as a whole. Transitions effectively link ideas and paragraphs.	offers no forecasting elements to govern sequencing of subtopics, so body paragraph sequencing seems uncontrolled or random, with insufficient or confusing transitional, organizational cues being employed.	thought, and the essay employs inadequate or misleading transitional devices or organizational cues.
Style and structure	Design of introductory, body, and concluding elements engages the audience's favorable attention and guides it through the essay's content, arranged in coherent body paragraphs that fully frame each perspective, clearly establish and support the writer's perspective, and	The introduction addresses the topic, sets the tone, and guides the reader into the body of the paper, which is developed in multiple separate paragraphs. A functional conclusion is present. The writing employs some variety of sentence pattern, and sentence construction is competent.	The essay uses spacing or indention, but paragraphs are not built around sound paragraphing principles and lack unity and coherence. A separate body and conclusion may not be included. Sentences are unclear, employing faulty or mixed constructions, with little or	Paragraphing is absent with sentences placed together without a discernible strategy. Introductory or concluding elements are inadequate, misleading, or omitted altogether. Sentences are difficult to interpret; grammar and paragraph structure are uncontrolled.

	Exceeds expectations	Meets expectations	Needs improvement	Does not meet expectations
Style and structure	refute opposing views and counterevidence. A conclusion reinforces the writer's position on the topic or promotes new insight. The paper achieves variety in sentence pattern and type. If using sources, the writer uses signal phrasing and clearly sets off cited from original material. Tone is skillfully controlled; word choice is apt, establishing the writer's credibility.	Sources used are acknowledged, but signal phrasing or parenthetical elements may be misplaced or lead to confusion. Diction is appropriate to audience or purpose, so the writer establishes credibility, but it may be eroded by repetitive or imprecise word choice.	no variety in pattern or type. No in-text citations are used to reference outside material, or they do not clearly distinguish the original work from cited material. Tone and diction are uncontrolled or inappropriate for the purpose and audience, so the writer's credibility is not fully established.	Sources, if used, are unacknowledged, resulting in plagiarism. Tone and diction are confusing, contradictory, or inappropriate, so the writer fails to establish credibility.
Precision and editing	The essay reveals mastery of all elements of grammar, usage, and mechanical conventions. Any outside sources are cited using proper bibliographic form. Formatting conventions for use of font and line spacing, use of headings, headers and footers, are applied	The essay is largely but not entirely free of grammatical, punctuation, and mechanical errors. Sentences are coherent, and structural errors (where present) do not disrupt the reading. Proper bibliographic form and mechanical conventions are employed to cite sources, with only	The essay is weakened with frequent errors in grammar, punctuation, and the use of mechanical conventions. References to outside sources are formatted incorrectly, sometimes leading to ambiguity of source or source type. The sub-mission may be	Sentence structure is not adequately controlled. Punctuation does not follow established convention. Bibliographic entries for outside sources are omitted or incomplete, and formatting conventions for citing sources are not followed. Illegible writing

Exceeds expectations	Meets expectations	Needs improvement	Does not meet expectations
appropriately throughout. Design elements direct the reader through each page. The writer executes the assignment memorably with no careless errors.	minor lapses in form or format. The paper is neat, legible, and clear, with formatting of manuscript conventions applied consistently. The paper satisfies the assignment with only scattered careless errors.	crumpled, stained, or torn. Errors in manuscript formatting conventions draw unfavorable attention. The writer attempts but fails to fully execute the assignment. Numerous editing errors distract, though perhaps cause only minor confusion.	is confusing. Stains, rips, blots, or printing errors may make parts of the paper unreadable. The writer fails to observe manuscript conventions or to satisfy other demands of the assignment. Errors throughout are serious enough to cause confusion and misunderstanding of meaning.

Gathering Responses and Collecting Your Thoughts

Gather all the reviewers' responses. Make notes about what you and your reviewers agree and disagree on, moving from most important issues, such as appropriateness of the topic, the persuasiveness of evidence and examples, the organization, and the support for ideas, to least important, such as spelling and comma placement. List areas where you agree that improvement is needed, and make a plan about what you need to revise. Think about areas of disagreement too. You make the final decisions about what changes to make, so determine which comments you need to respond to and which you can ignore.

REVISION AND EDITING ACTIVITIES

Identifying Options for Revision Planning

After you have gathered revision comments on your early draft from peer reviewers and your instructor (pp. 195–96), choose one of the following strategies to begin making your revision plan.

- Create a storyboard. On a sticky note or note card, write your argumentative thesis and put it at the top of your work area. Using separate sticky notes or note cards for each paragraph or example, write down important features such as topic sentences, research sources, and supporting details. Does your organization make sense? Do the parts work together? Does every paragraph help to advance the story and clarify the point it makes? Using sticky notes or note cards of a different color, add notes to each paragraph about how you will strengthen, change, or delete content based on your reviewers' comments and your own. Take photos of the parts of the storyboard so you'll have a record of what you decide, even if you lose your notes.

- Create a graphic organizer. Using either paper and pencil or a digital document, create text boxes representing each introductory paragraph, body paragraph, and conclusion paragraph, and write the main idea of each paragraph in the box. Below it, leave room to revise the main idea. To the right of each main idea box, draw additional boxes for changes, additions, and deletions you have decided to make to supporting details, transitions, and other material in that paragraph.

- Make an annotated outline. Using formal complete sentences or informal phrases, make an outline that shows the current main ideas, supporting details, and organization of your draft. Using highlighters, colored pens, different colors of type, or some other method to make your changes clearly visible, annotate your outline to show the changes you plan to make to your thesis, dominant impression, organization, supporting ideas, introduction, conclusion, references, and so on.

- Make a plan of your own. _____
_____
_____
_____
_____

Revising an Argument Essay

Following the plan you've created, write a complete revised draft. Repeat as needed until you feel that you have a solid draft that is nearly final.

Using Your Common Issues to Focus Editing of Your Argument Essay

Edit for grammar, punctuation, and other common problems you have.

- The two kinds of problems that teachers or peer reviewers point out most often in my writing are _____ and
_____.

- I know I sometimes struggle with _____.
- The citation issues I notice most often include _____
_____.

Review the information in Part 3 (pp. 205–42) about the errors you have identified above. Then reread your draft again, correcting any such errors and other issues that you find.

Proofreading

- Run the spell-checker and carefully consider every suggestion. Do not automatically accept the suggestions! Remember that spell-checkers cannot identify problems with certain kinds of words, such as homonyms and proper nouns (names), so check the spelling of such words yourself. Write the words you have misspelled on a spelling checklist you can use to identify and avoid words that give you trouble.
- Read your essay aloud slowly, noting and correcting any issues that you find.
- Read your essay aloud backward, word by word, looking for repeated words and similar mistakes that are easy to miss in work that is very familiar. Correct any problems you see.

When your work is as error-free and professional as you can make it, submit your essay.

PART THREE

ADDITIONAL TOOLS FOR PRACTICE

14 Sentence Guides for Academic Writers   207

15 Writing Grammatically Correct Sentences   218

16 Writing Clear Sentences in a Thoughtful Style   225

17 Activities for Improving Your Writing   239

14

SENTENCE GUIDES FOR ACADEMIC WRITERS

Being a college student means being a college writer. No matter what field you are studying, your instructors will ask you to make sense of what you are learning through writing. When you work on writing assignments in college, you are, in most cases, being asked to write for an academic audience.

Writing academically means thinking academically — asking a lot of questions, digging into the ideas of others, and entering into scholarly debates and academic conversations. As a college writer, you will be asked to read different kinds of texts; understand and evaluate authors' ideas, arguments, and methods; and contribute your own ideas. In this way, you present yourself as a participant in an academic conversation.

What does it mean to be part of an *academic conversation*? Well, think of it this way: You and your friends may have an ongoing debate about the best film trilogy of all time. During your conversations with one another, you analyze the details of the films, introduce points you want your friends to consider, listen to their ideas, and perhaps cite what the critics have said about a particular trilogy. This kind of conversation is not unlike what happens among scholars in academic writing — except they could be debating the best public policy for a social problem or the most promising new theory in treating disease.

If you are uncertain about what academic writing *sounds like* or if you're not sure you're any good at it, this chapter offers guidance for you at the sentence level. It helps answer questions such as these:

How can I present the ideas of others in a way that demonstrates my understanding of the debate?

How can I agree with someone, but add a new idea?

How can I disagree with a scholar without seeming, well, rude?

How can I make clear in my writing which ideas are mine and which ideas are someone else's?

The following sections offer sentence guides for you to use and adapt to your own writing situations. As in all writing that you do, you will have to think about your purpose (reason for writing) and your audience (readers) before knowing which guides will be most appropriate for a particular piece of writing or for a certain part of your essay.

The guides are organized to help you present background information, the views and claims of others, and your own views and claims—all in the context of your purpose and audience.

ACADEMIC WRITERS PRESENT INFORMATION AND OTHERS' VIEWS

When you write in academic situations, you may be asked to spend some time giving background information for or setting a context for your main idea or argument. This often requires you to present or summarize what is known or what has already been said in relation to the question you are asking in your writing.

Presenting What Is Known or Assumed

When you write, you will find that you occasionally need to present something that is known, such as a specific fact or a statistic. The following structures are useful when you are providing background information.

- As we know from history, _____.
- X has shown that _____.
- Research by X and Y suggests that _____.

- According to X, _____ percent of _____ are/favor _____.

In other situations, you may have the need to present information that is assumed or that is conventional wisdom.

- People often believe that _____.
- Conventional wisdom leads us to believe _____.
- Many Americans share the idea that _____.
- _____ is a widely held belief.

In order to challenge an assumption or a widely held belief, you have to acknowledge it first. Doing so lets your readers believe that you are placing your ideas in an appropriate context.

- Although many people are led to believe X, there is a significant benefit to considering the merits of Y.
- College students tend to believe that _____ when, in fact, _____.

Presenting Others' Views

As a writer, you build your own *ethos*, or credibility, by being able to fairly and accurately represent the views of others. As an academic writer, you will be expected to demonstrate your understanding of a text by summarizing the views or arguments of its author(s). To do so, you will use language such as the following.

- X argues that _____.
- X emphasizes the need for _____.
- In this important article, X and Y claim _____
_____.
- X endorses _____ because _____.
- X and Y have recently criticized the idea that _____.
- _____, according to X, is the most critical cause of
_____.

Although you will create your own variations of these sentences as you draft and revise, the guides can be useful tools for thinking through how best to present another writer's claim or finding clearly and concisely.

Presenting Direct Quotations

When the exact words of a source are important for accuracy, authority, emphasis, or flavor, you will want to use a direct quotation. Ordinarily, you will present direct quotations with language of your own that suggests how you are using the source.

- X characterizes the problem this way: " . . . ".
- According to X, _____ is defined as " . . . ".
- " . . . ," explains X.
- X argues strongly in favor of the policy, pointing out that " . . . ".

Note: You will generally cite direct quotations according to the documentation style your readers expect. MLA style, often used in English and in other humanities courses, recommends using the author name paired with a page number, if there is one. APA style, used in most social sciences, requires the year of publication generally after the mention of the source, with page numbers after the quoted material. In *Chicago* style, used in history and in some humanities courses, writers use superscript numbers (like this[6]) to refer readers to footnotes or endnotes. In-text citations, like the ones shown below, refer readers to entries in the works-cited or reference list.

MLA	Lazarín argues that our overreliance on testing in K–12 schools "does not put students first" (20).
APA	Lazarín (2014) argues that our overreliance on testing in K–12 schools "does not put students first" (p. 20).
Chicago	Lazarín argues that our overreliance on testing in K–12 schools "does not put students first."[6]

Many writers use direct quotations to advance an argument of their own:

Standardized testing makes it easier for administrators to measure student performance, but it may not be the best way to measure it. Too much testing wears students out and communicates the idea that recall is the most important skill we want them to develop. Even education policy adviser Melissa Lazarín argues that our overreliance on testing in K–12 schools "does not put students first" (20).

Student writer's idea

Source's idea

Presenting Alternative Views

Most debates, whether they are scholarly or popular, are complex—often with more than two sides to an issue. Sometimes you will have to synthesize the views of multiple participants in the debate before you introduce your own ideas.

- On the one hand, X reports that _____, but on the other hand, Y insists that _____.
- Even though X endorses the policy, Y refers to it as " . . . "
- X, however, isn't convinced and instead argues _____.
- X and Y have supported the theory in the past, but new research by Z suggests that _____.

ACADEMIC WRITERS PRESENT THEIR OWN VIEWS

When you write for an academic audience, you will indeed have to demonstrate that you are familiar with the views of others who are asking the same kinds of questions as you are. Much writing that is done for academic purposes asks you to put your arguments in the context of existing arguments—in a way asking you to connect the known to the new.

When you are asked to write a summary or an informative text, your own views and arguments are generally not called for. However, much of the writing you will be assigned to do in college asks you to take a persuasive stance and present a reasoned argument—at times in response to a single text and at other times in response to multiple texts.

Presenting Your Own Views: Agreement and Extension

Sometimes you agree with the author of a source.

- X's argument is convincing because _____.
- Because X's approach is so _____, it is the best way to _____.
- X makes an important point when she says _____.

Other times you find you agree with the author of a source, but you want to extend the point or go a bit deeper in your own investigation. In a way, you acknowledge the source for getting you so far in the conversation, but then you move the conversation along with a related comment or finding.

- X's proposal for _____ is indeed worth considering. Going one step further, _____.
- X makes the claim that _____. By extension, isn't it also true, then, that _____?
- _____ has been adequately explained by X. Now, let's move beyond that idea and ask whether _____.

Presenting Your Own Views: Queries and Skepticism

You may be intimidated when you're asked to talk back to a source, especially if the source is a well-known scholar or expert or even just a frequent voice in a particular debate. College-level writing asks you to be skeptical, however, and approach academic questions with the mind of an investigator. It is acceptable to doubt, to question, to challenge — as the result is often new knowledge or understanding about a subject.

- Couldn't it also be argued that _____?
- But is everyone willing to agree that this is the case?
- While X insists that _____ is so, he/she is perhaps asking the wrong question to begin with.
- The claims that X and Y have made, while intelligent and well-meaning, leave many unconvinced because they have failed to consider _____.

Presenting Your Own Views: Disagreement or Correction

You may find that at times the only response you have to a text or to an author is complete disagreement.

- X's claims about _____ are completely misguided.
- X presents a long metaphor comparing _____ to _____; in the end, the comparison is unconvincing because _____.

It can be tempting to disregard a source completely if you detect a piece of information that strikes you as false or that you know to be untrue.

- Although X reports that _____, recent studies indicate that is not the case.
- While X and Y insist that _____ is so, an examination of their figures shows that they have made an important miscalculation.

> **A NOTE ABOUT USING THE FIRST PERSON ("I")**
>
> Some disciplines look favorably upon the use of the first person "I" in academic writing. Others do not and instead stick to using the third person. If you are given a writing assignment for a class, you are better off asking your instructor what he or she prefers or reading through any samples given than *guessing* what might be expected.
>
> **FIRST PERSON (I, ME, MY, WE, US, OUR)**
>
> > I question Heddinger's methods and small sample size.
> >
> > Harnessing children's technology obsession in the classroom is, I believe, the key to improving learning.
> >
> > Lanza's interpretation focuses on circle imagery as symbolic of the family; my analysis leads me in a different direction entirely.
> >
> > We would, in fact, benefit from looser laws about farming on our personal property.
>
> **THIRD PERSON (NAMES AND OTHER NOUNS)**
>
> > Heddinger's methods and small sample size are questionable.
> >
> > Harnessing children's technology obsession in the classroom is the key to improving learning.
> >
> > Lanza's interpretation focuses on circle imagery as symbolic of the family; other readers' analyses may point in a different direction entirely.
> >
> > Many Americans would, in fact, benefit from looser laws about farming on personal property.
>
> You may feel that not being able to use "I" in an essay in which you present your ideas about a topic is unfair or will lead to weaker statements. Know that you can make a strong argument even if you write in the third person.

Presenting and Countering Objections to Your Argument

Effective college writers know that their arguments are stronger when they can anticipate objections that others might make.

- Some will object to this proposal on the grounds that _____.

- Not everyone will embrace _____; they may argue instead that _____.

Countering, or responding to, opposing voices fairly and respectfully strengthens your writing and your *ethos*, or credibility.

- X and Y might contend that this interpretation is faulty; however, _____.
- Most _____ believe that there is too much risk in this approach. But what they have failed to take into consideration is _____.

ACADEMIC WRITERS PERSUADE BY PUTTING IT ALL TOGETHER

Readers of academic writing often want to know what's at stake in a particular debate or text. They want to know why it is that they should care and that they should keep reading. Aside from crafting individual sentences, you must, of course, keep the bigger picture in mind as you attempt to persuade, inform, evaluate, or review.

Presenting Stakeholders

When you write, you may be doing so as a member of a group affected by the research conversation you have entered. For example, you may be among the thousands of students in your state whose level of debt may change as a result of new laws about financing a college education. In this case, you are a *stakeholder* in the matter. In other words, you have an interest in the matter as a person who could be impacted by the outcome of a decision. On the other hand, you may be writing as an investigator of a topic that interests you but that you aren't directly connected with. You may be persuading your audience on behalf of a group of interested stakeholders—a group of which you yourself are not a member.

You can give your writing some teeth if you make it clear who is being affected by the discussion of the issue and the decisions that have been or will be made about the issue. The groups of stakeholders are highlighted in the following sentences.

- Viewers of Kurosawa's films may not agree with X that _____.
- The research will come as a surprise to parents of children with Type 1 diabetes.
- X's claims have the power to offend potentially every low-wage earner in the state.
- Marathoners might want to reconsider their training regimen if stories such as those told by X and Y are validated by the medical community.

Presenting the "So What"

For readers to be motivated to read your writing, they have to feel as if you're addressing something that matters to them, addressing something that matters very much to you, or addressing something that should matter to us all. Good academic writing often hooks readers with a sense of urgency—a serious response to a reader's "So what?"

- Having a frank discussion about _____ now will put us in a far better position to deal with _____ in the future. If we are unwilling or unable to do so, we risk _____.

- Such a breakthrough will affect _____ in three significant ways.

- It is easy to believe that the stakes aren't high enough to be alarming; in fact, _____ will be affected by _____.

- Widespread disapproval of and censorship of such fiction/films/art will mean _____ for us in the future. Culture should represent _____.

- _____ could bring about unprecedented opportunities to participate in _____, something never seen before.

- New experimentation in _____ could allow scientists to investigate _____ in ways they couldn't have imagined _____ years ago.

Presenting the Players and Positions in a Debate

Some disciplines ask writers to compose a review of the literature as a part of a larger project—or sometimes as a freestanding assignment. In a review of the literature, the writer sets forth a research question, summarizes the key sources that have addressed the question, puts the current research in the context of other voices in the research conversation, and identifies any gaps in the research.

Writing that presents a debate, its players, and their positions can often be lengthy. What follows, however, can give you the sense of the flow of ideas and turns in such a piece of writing.

_____ affects more than 30 percent of children in America, and signs point to a worsening situation in years to come because of A, B, and C. Solutions to the problem have eluded even the sharpest policy minds and brightest researchers. In an important 2003 study, W found that _____, which pointed to more problems than solutions. [. . .] Research by X and Y made strides in our

Student writer states the problem.

Student writer summarizes the views of others on the topic.

understanding of _____ *but still didn't offer specific strategies for children and families struggling to* _____. [. . .] *When Z rejected both the methods and the findings of X and Y, arguing that* _____, *policymakers and health care experts were optimistic.* [. . .] *Too much discussion of* _____, *however, and too little discussion of* _____, *may lead us to solutions that are ultimately too expensive to sustain.*

Student writer presents her view in the context of current research.

Using Appropriate Signal Verbs

Verbs matter. Using a variety of verbs in your sentences can add strength and clarity as you present others' views and your own views.

WHEN YOU WANT TO PRESENT A VIEW FAIRLY NEUTRALLY

acknowledges	observes
adds	points out
admits	reports
comments	suggests
contends	writes
notes	

- X points out that the plan had unintended outcomes.

WHEN YOU WANT TO PRESENT A STRONGER VIEW

argues	emphasizes
asserts	insists
declares	

- Y argues in favor of a ban on _____; but Z insists the plan is misguided.

WHEN YOU WANT TO SHOW AGREEMENT

agrees
confirms
endorses

- An endorsement of X's position is smart for a number of reasons.

WHEN YOU WANT TO SHOW CONTRAST OR DISAGREEMENT

compares   refutes
denies   rejects
disputes

- The town must come together and reject X's claims that _____ is in the best interest of the citizens.

WHEN YOU WANT TO ANTICIPATE AN OBJECTION

admits
acknowledges
concedes

- Y admits that closer study of _____, with a much larger sample size, is necessary for _____.

15

WRITING GRAMMATICALLY CORRECT SENTENCES

CORRECTING SENTENCE BOUNDARY ISSUES

Sometimes we need to set personal boundaries in life. Have you ever been in a particularly clingy relationship where a friend or a person you are dating only wants to spend time with you and maybe even acts like you are one and the same person? Depending on your personality and needs, you might have brought the issue to the person's attention and said that you needed space to be your own person. This means you set a personal boundary. Sentences need boundaries too. They need to be complete on their own, and they need appropriate space from other sentences to communicate their full meaning.

What is often tricky about sentence boundaries is that they are based in grammatical rules and not whatever you might think is logical. If you haven't spent a lot of time reading books, articles, and other print materials and observing how sentences function in them, you will need to learn how sentences function grammatically to understand their boundaries and how to write them with confidence. Do not despair! In the age of social media, there is mass confusion about what makes up a complete sentence, and many would argue that the rules will eventually change to meet our evolving needs. For now, here are some activities to help you learn how to set sentence boundaries correctly.

Correcting Sentence Boundary Issues

Activities

Take a look at the sentences below and circle which is correct:

1. I often go to parties with my friends, my friends are more social than I am.
2. I often go to parties with my friends; my friends are more social than I am.
3. I often go to parties with my friends, but my friends are more social than I am.

The final sentence might be the best option, but both of the last two sentences are grammatically correct. Some students think that the first is correct because the topic stays the same throughout the sentence. You are writing about friends and parties the whole time, so that should be a complete sentence, right? In other languages, such as Japanese, sentences are arranged by topic, but this is not true in English. The first sentence is a type of run-on sentence called a comma splice. It is missing the appropriate punctuation, instead splicing together two complete thoughts with only a comma. These two complete thoughts need better boundaries than what a comma provides.

In order to have a complete sentence, you need to have at least one complete thought, at least one verb, and at least one subject. Grammatically speaking, a "complete thought" is what we call an **independent clause**. It's independent because, much like an independent person with good boundaries, it is complete and can stand alone. "I often go to parties with my friends" is an independent clause because it has a subject ("I"), a verb ("go"), and is a complete thought that can stand alone as its own complete sentence. Likewise, "My friends are more social than I am" is also an independent clause because it has a subject ("My friends"), a verb ("are"), and is a complete thought that can stand alone as its own complete sentence as well.

If you have two separate independent clauses, such as in this example, and they are fused together (meaning, no punctuation divides them) or spliced together with a comma (as in example 1), they form a **run-on sentence**, which means they have poor boundaries and are grammatically incorrect.

To put two or more independent clauses into a single complete sentence requires the use of either a **conjunction** (such as *and*, *but*, *for*, *or*, or *so*) preceded by a comma (example 3) or a stronger linking punctuation mark than a comma (such as a colon or a semicolon, as in example 2). When two independent clauses are properly joined, as in examples 2 and 3 above, they unite to form a complete sentence.

Relatedly, if you have a grouping of words that forms an incomplete thought, is missing a verb, or is missing a subject, you have a **sentence fragment**. For example, "Parties with my friends," is a sentence fragment. Most obviously, it is missing a verb and is not a complete thought. It raises too many questions. It cannot stand alone as an independent clause, and it cannot stand alone as a complete sentence. Let's define these terms simply.

A **subject** is what is being or doing the verb ("*I often go . . .*").

A **verb** is a state of being experienced by the subject or action done by the subject ("I often *go* . . .").

An **independent clause** is a complete thought that contains, at the very least, a subject and a verb. It can stand alone as a complete sentence.

A **run-on sentence** joins two independent clauses incorrectly, causing sentence boundary confusion.

A **conjunction** is a linking word, such as *and*, *but*, or *or*, that can be used to join two clauses.

A **dependent clause** has a subject and a verb, but it is an incomplete thought and therefore cannot stand alone. Consider the independent clause, "I often go to parties with my friends." If it had a word like *while* at its start, it would become dependent on more information to make it complete: "While I often go to parties with my friends." That clause no longer stands alone; it is dependent.

A **sentence fragment** is when a dependent clause or any other kind of incomplete thought is incorrectly treated as if it were complete. A sentence fragment is never a complete sentence.

Another term you need to know is **prepositional phrase**, since prepositional phrases can get in the way of you identifying subjects and verbs. A prepositional phrase contains a preposition that often shows where something is or when it is.

Identifying Subjects and Verbs

Circle the subjects and underline the verbs in the sentences below and write down why you selected your answers:

1. In life we often set personal boundaries.
2. Sentences have boundaries too.
3. Some students think that the first sentence is correct because the topic stays the same throughout the sentence.
4. The first sentence is a run-on sentence.
5. It is missing the appropriate punctuation.
6. The verb is sometimes the action in the sentence.
7. I want to get better at correcting errors.
8. I love grammar.
9. On Tuesdays, I go to the learning lab.
10. I left my paper on my bed.

The Implied You

One common area of confusion that students often struggle with relates to the "implied you."

Often when there is a command, the subject, you, is implied rather than explicitly written down.

For example, one might say, "Sit down." This is a complete sentence because the "you" being spoken to is clearly implied and therefore, for all intents and purposes, present in the sentence.

Look at the "implied you" sentences below and identify the verb.

1. Sit down.
2. Stand up.
3. Go for a walk.
4. Know that I love you.
5. Sing loudly.

Correcting Sentence Fragments

Now that you know what a complete thought, verb, and subject are, you can correct the sentence fragments below. Remember that the minimum one needs for a complete sentence is a subject (clearly implied or explicitly stated), a verb, and a complete thought. These sentence fragments lack a complete thought, a subject, a verb, or a combination of these.

Correct each sentence fragment below. Explain why you corrected it as you did.

1. The minimum one needs.
2. Now that you know.
3. Correcting sentence fragments.
4. Susan.
5. Which is why it's important to proofread your papers.
6. The reason why I struggle with grammar.
7. Because I often procrastinate.
8. Into the paper.

Your Sentences

Write down ten sentences from a recent paper you wrote. Identify the subjects, verbs, and complete thoughts in your sentences. Next, note if any of the sentences are run-ons or fragments. It's fine if they are perfectly correct sentences! This is just an opportunity to look at your sentences in isolation from the rest of your paper. Why do you think it might be a good idea to look at your sentences in isolation from the rest of your paper?

Run-Ons and Fragments in Context

Look at the paragraph below, and highlight all run-ons and fragments. Then rewrite the paragraph correctly.

> Kimberly, a student at Community College of Philadelphia, was brilliant. But she wasn't very good at identifying run-ons and fragments. It seemed to her that her sentences were fine because they made sense when she read the whole paper, no one really taught her grammar rules either. Which made her really frustrated. One day Kimberly went to the learning lab and learned the rules for correcting sentences. And fragments. She was overjoyed. On her next paper, she still had a lot of run-on and fragment errors but not as many. Be like Kimberly! When you struggle with your writing, don't be afraid to ask for help. Even if you usually don't need it.

Run-Ons and Fragments in the Real World

Go outside your classroom, dorm room, break room, or wherever you are right now, and look at the kinds of sentences you see on signs, buildings, fliers, and the like. Note three run-on sentences you find in the world. Then note three sentence fragments. Now write each incorrect run-on sentence and sentence fragment. Beneath each, please correct the sentence so that it is a complete sentence with appropriate boundaries. Sometimes these errors are intentional, as in a paper that says *For Sale* as a title, and sometimes they are not intentional, as in *Call me, I have a great Math 116 textbook for only $60.*

Pronouns

Pronouns like *I, you, he, she, it, we, they, this,* or *that* are wonderful because they mean we do not have to keep saying the noun over and over and over again. Pronouns help us avoid situations like this:

Students often have to stand in line at financial aid. Students may not want to do this because they have to attend to their studies. Students sometimes do not have a choice.

In these sentences, using the word *they* for students would help create some variety.

Sometimes, if there are multiple nouns in a sentence or the opposite—no clear noun that the pronoun is referring to—you can confuse your reader.

Look at the examples below, then complete the activity.

Students often have to go to the financial aid window where the financial aid officers are in charge of answering questions. They can get frustrated.

The pronoun that is challenging here is *they*. Does *they* refer to the financial aid officers or the students? It may be that both are true, but as a writer you have to make clear what you mean. Here are two options for correcting the sentence above.

Students often have to go to the financial aid window where the financial aid officers are in charge of answering questions. Students can get frustrated.

or

Students often have to go to the financial aid window where the financial aid officers are in charge of answering questions. Both students and financial aid officers can get frustrated.

Another problem that often arises in papers is the nebulous (unclear) use of *this* or *that*. Imagine that you have just discussed various philosophers' points about ethics. You end your paragraph with:

This shows that there is no precise definition for ethics.

Do you mean the varying ideas of all the philosophers you spoke about in the paragraph? The ideas of the last philosopher you talked about? Your ideas? In this instance, you need to substitute *this* for a clear noun or group of nouns so your reader knows what you are referring to.

Look at the sentences below. Circle or highlight the confusing pronoun or pronouns and then rewrite the sentence with a more specific noun or nouns.

EXAMPLE:

- Original sentence: Reports give your readers information about various topics. They may or may not be familiar to your reader.

    Rewritten sentence: <u>Reports give your readers information about various topics. The topics may or may not be familiar to your reader.</u>

1. There are different types of love according to the ancient philosophers. This is true today.

2. Revisions are important because they help you to communicate your ideas. They can often be unclear at first.

3. Lin-Manuel Miranda wrote *Hamilton* after reading a book about Alexander Hamilton. To many, he is considered a genius.

4. Oftentimes, people think of gender as something fixed at birth, but it really is a social construct. That is the problem.

5. Professors could do a better job meeting the evolving needs of students. They often forget how emotionally overwhelming college can be.

6. Dan doesn't really like his pet turtle. He makes a lot of noise at night.

7. Students often want to do well, but they don't know the steps to take for writing essays. These can be daunting.

8. You might focus your binoculars on a whale in the distance or you may be interested in pointing your binoculars toward a boat party to spy on it! It is different in each of these instances.

9. It may feel helpful when someone tells you the answers to grammar questions or math problems, but they don't always stick unless you learn how to find them on your own.

10. They often write essays in the first person. It is a good strategy for writing narrative essays, but they sometimes have a hard time transitioning to more objective writing for reports.

Pronouns in Your Work

Find an essay or short piece of writing that you have completed. Write down two consecutive sentences that have pronouns in them or one sentence that has a noun followed by another sentence with a pronoun. Identify the nouns/pronouns and tell why your pronoun references are clear or whether you should revise them. Please note that you do not need to find sentences with errors for this activity. The act of identifying pronouns in two consecutive sentences in your work will help to prime your brain to check for pronoun references the next time you write.

16

WRITING CLEAR SENTENCES IN A THOUGHTFUL STYLE

SENTENCE COMBINATION

The way sentences are constructed dictates how readers engage with our work. More complex sentences challenge the reader's mind. Shorter sentences can give them a short break to process information. Sentences constructed entirely in the same way can be overwhelming to your readers and might make them put down your essay. Therefore, it's good to practice the skill of sentence combination so that you are able to create sentence variety in your papers.

Look at the same example from the pronoun section on p. 223:

Students often have to go to the financial aid window where the financial aid officers are in charge of answering questions. Students can get frustrated.

These two sentences can be combined into a smoother sentence in a variety of ways. Here are some options:

Students often have to go to the financial aid window where the financial aid officers are in charge of answering questions, and students can get frustrated.

This option simply uses the conjunction *and* to add information to the sentence. It emphasizes the word *students* by repeating it. The sentence gives the reader a sense that students are the most important preoccupation of the reader and perhaps subtly implies the severity of the financial aid officers' impact on students.

Students can get frustrated when they have to go to the financial aid window where financial aid officers are supposed to answer their questions.

This option places the frustration first and shifts the sentence slightly to be about how the officers are supposed to answer questions but likely don't. The emphasis in this sentence is less on the students and more on the challenges that the financial aid officers pose to students.

Financial aid workers, the people in charge of answering student questions, can often frustrate students.

This option puts financial aid workers' job title as the subject and focuses mainly on how their actions frustrate students.

The distinctions are very subtle, but as a writer, you have complete control over how you want your thoughts to be perceived. All of these options are valid, and they will add texture to your paper. They will also help you to shape your emphasis at any given moment. Think about the various methods for sentence combination and complete the activity below.

Activity

Write down what you believe is the most effective combination of each pair of sentences below.

1. The student wanted to do a good job. He was only a freshman and didn't have the same skills as his peers.
2. Sometimes, the scholars disagree on definitions of terms. The way you define something can change your perception of it.
3. Lin-Manuel Miranda liked hip-hop as a child. Lin-Manuel Miranda's father was a political consultant.
4. A research report is an objective essay that presents information on a topic that you have investigated. It is not a personal essay.
5. An infographic is a report that includes visual elements. For example, you might include graphics of cigarettes if you are creating an infographic about smoking on campus.
6. Explanations give information to answer *how*, *why*, or *what* questions. They do not simply present information.
7. A causal analysis speculates potential reasons for a problem or phenomenon. A causal analysis also uses research to back up the speculations.

8. One point of an argument is to help people think in new ways about topics. Another point is to create solutions to issues in the world.//
9. A proposal provides your readers with one or more solutions to a problem. It can also provide ideas for how to handle a situation or suggestions for the allocation of funds.
10. Below is a list of steps for creating an exploratory essay. Each activity is intended to get you thinking about what to do for each step.

SENTENCE COMBINATION IN YOUR WORK

Activity

Write down three pairs of sentences from a recent essay you have written. Practice combining the sentences after you write down the originals.

SUBJECT/VERB AGREEMENT

In English, subjects and verbs have to agree in number. In other words, you should not have a singular subject like *he* paired with a plural verb like *know*. In order to understand this concept, please read the following and then complete the activity.

We have the following pronouns or words that stand in for nouns:

Singular (one)

I

You

He/She/It

Plural (more than one)

We

They

Infinitives

An infinitive is the pure form of the verb. In English, an infinitive always has the word "to" before it. "To swim" is the infinitive and "I swim" is first person singular. The infinitive "to be" can never be used in academic written English as a conjugation. Example: *You are happy* instead of *You be happy.*

Third Person Singular

In academic written English, remember to include an "s" in the third person singular construction.

EXAMPLES:
- She walks to the store.
- Mary knows the answer.
- There she goes.

CONJUGATIONS

If you are ever unsure of how to make a subject and verb agree, look up the following in a search engine: "English conjugation of the infinitive _____." Example: "English conjugation of the infinitive to go." In addition to any verb conjugations you may have trouble with, please memorize the following:

To Be (present tense → happening now)

I am
You are
He/She/It is
We are
They are

To Be (past tense → happened then)

I was
You were
He/She/It was
We were
They were

To Have (present tense → happening now)

I have
You have
He/She/It has
We have
They have

To Have (past tense → happened then)

I had
You had
He/She/It had
We had
They had

To Go (present tense → happening now)

I go
You go
He/She/It goes
We go
They go

To Go (past tense → happened then)

I went
You went
He/She/It went
We went
They went

Activity

Now correct the subject/verb errors in the sentences below. All of the sentences should remain in the present tense. The present tense tells what is happening now.

1. She go to the store.
2. The dog walk every day.
3. They reads many books.
4. The weather be intense.
5. The student learn very easily.
6. We knows the answer.
7. The stars, in the sky, is visible.
8. The snowflake fall on my nose.

9. You asks too many questions.
10. One way to be happy are by reading.

VOCABULARY DEVELOPMENT IN PAPERS

There are many ways to improve your vocabulary and the strategy that many college students choose is to look up synonyms (words that mean the same thing) in a thesaurus. The problem with this method is that, oftentimes, the words don't mean exactly the same thing. If you have never used the word before, you will be missing subtle denotations and connotations of the words. In other words, the new potentially "bigger" word you choose will be communicating something different from what you'd like to communicate. First, answer the following questions about this paragraph and your vocabulary development process. Then, complete the activity.

1. What is *denotation*?
2. What is *connotation*?
3. When you want to increase your vocabulary in general, what do you personally do and why?
4. When you want to improve your vocabulary in your papers, what do you do and why?

Activity

One way to try out new words that works really well is using words you have seen or heard before. You are likely reading books or articles that have *new* words in them. By *new*, I do not necessarily mean words you've never *seen* before, but I do mean words you have never *used* before. Go back into one or more books or articles that you have read for this class and find some vocabulary words you personally have not used from these sources. List them out. After the word, write, in quotation marks, the sentence where it appeared in the book or article. Write the dictionary definition of the word that is closest to the meaning in the sentence where it appears. Then write your own sentence with the word.

Activity

Try to incorporate two of the words from the previous activity into your next paper. In order to do that, write your topic and then brainstorm possible sentences that might contain the vocabulary word. For example, let's say the topic of your next paper is homelessness and one of your vocabulary words is "obfuscate." You might write the following sample sentence:

Sometimes existing resources for homeless people obfuscate the problems that still exist for homeless populations.

Notice that the practice sentence contains the word "homeless," which is part of your theme. It also contains your vocabulary word. You don't need to force the exact sentences you write into your paper, but it's helpful to think about possible sentences before you write the next paper. That way, your brain is primed to try to use a few new words.

Once you've completed the activity, ask yourself: Did this process work for you? If so, why? If not, what other techniques might you try?

SPECIFICITY AND PRECISION OF LANGUAGE

Sometimes people feel that specificity and precision of language is reserved for personal and narrative essays or other forms of creative writing. You can certainly hone your precision skills through practicing these forms of writing, and in fact, the first activity below is going to ask you to do just that! However, specificity and precision of language is important for every type of essay you write. Even if you are writing a research report, the language you use and the specificity of your details can make a difference between an A paper and a C paper. It can make a difference in your reader understanding what you are saying or putting your paper down. The stakes can be higher than you think! The activities below are intended to help you develop precision in your language.

Has a teacher ever written "be specific" in the margins of your paper? If so, how did you react? Do you think you are good at using specific, precise words in your paper or is this something you need to work on? Explain why or why not.

Activity

The haiku is a form of creative writing that was invented in Japan. It is a poetic form that often has a prescribed set of syllables or voiced vowel sounds in each line. Haiku are short sensory glimpses into the world. One of the main reasons why writing a couple of haiku can help you with attention to language and precision is that they are very short. Unlike your papers that are pages long, many haiku follow the pattern of five syllables (line 1), seven syllables (line 2), and then five syllables (line 3). Contemporary haiku do not always follow that exact pattern. Look at the following sample haiku by contemporary haiku poet Barry George, which has a different syllabic pattern but the same three lines and a more traditional second line. After reading Barry George's poems, complete the activities.

> after the storm
> he is rich in umbrellas—
> the homeless man

> off to school
> a father and two
> little umbrellas

1. What image or object appears in both poems? How does it appear differently in both poems?
2. Which of the five senses do these poems most appeal to? How do you know?

Activity

1. What is an object that is near you right now that is interesting to you or one about which you have a strong opinion? For example, does your mechanical pencil keep breaking? Is someone's bright red sweater still hanging on the hook in the back of the room? Write that object here.
2. Write one or more haiku about that object. Be as specific as possible.
3. Now take any three lines of a recent essay and turn them into a haiku using the traditional syllabic pattern.
4. Look at your haiku. What do you need to add to make it more interesting? What might you need to take away?
5. Revise your haiku.

DESCRIPTION AND PARAGRAPH EXPANSION

In order to describe objects, moments, or ideas, it is a good idea to use specific language. The following activity is designed to get you thinking about how to describe specifically and how to expand your paragraphs without just "padding" them for the sake of hitting page quotas.

To describe, think of the senses (touch, taste, smell, sight, hearing). Instead of saying *the bucket*, say *the blue bucket with the smooth handle that I found on my fourth birthday*.

To expand paragraphs, ask yourself *who, what, where, when, why* questions. For example, if you described a reason for a political policy, you might then talk about who was involved.

Activity

Select a photograph that speaks to you. Then write a paragraph that is as specific as possible that is about or inspired by that photograph.

Highlight two sentences that could be made more sensory and one sentence that could be expanded to answer *who, what, where, when, why, how* questions. Then rewrite the paragraph. Make sure it is more sensory and expanded.

Activity

Take a look at the sentences below and turn them into sentences that are more specific, following the example below.

Original Sentence: There are many homeless people in Philadelphia.

Revision A: Amid the hustle and bustle of shoppers on 17th and Walnut Street in Philadelphia, you will find corners speckled with homeless veterans asking for money.

Revision B: According to Project Home, there were 15,000 Philadelphians who used shelters in 2015 (Facts on Homelessness).

Note that the way you revise your sentences depends on the type of paper that you are writing. Sometimes you have to add precision through your language choices. As was true in your haiku, the first revision makes the sentence much more sensory and engaging. The second revision, appropriate for forms of writing like reports, explanations, and evaluations, adds specific information, in this case data about the use of shelters in Philadelphia.

1. **Original Sentence:** I walk home from school late at night.
2. **Original Sentence:** This college has a lot of extracurricular programs.
3. **Original Sentence:** In 2020 President Trump made a policy that impacted many people.
4. **Original Sentence:** The dollhouse was disturbing.
5. **Original Sentence:** The president of the college has more to do with student success or failure than you would think.
6. **Original Sentence:** *Wicked* is a good musical.
7. **Original Sentence:** The impact of the arts is widespread.
8. **Original Sentence:** The ladybug walked on my paper, and I had an idea.

9. **Original Sentence:** I learned to read because my mom made me.
10. **Original Sentence:** The best way to grow is to be open to changing your perspective.

Activity

Select a paper that you have written recently and write down at least five sentences that you might be able to revise. First write the type of paper it is and the conventions of that paper. In other words, can you revise your sentences using subjective information (opinion-based) or do you need to stick to the facts? Is there room for more creative and/or sensory sentences in this paper? After you have answered these questions, work on revising some of your sentences. Please note that you may want to steer away from the topic sentences (the first sentences of each paragraph) as they can often be intentionally general.

TRANSITIONS

Transitions help your reader get smoothly from one sentence to the other or one part of an essay to another. Sometimes you can use transition words to achieve this movement. Sometimes it is best to form a bridge between sentences instead of repeating the language in one sentence in the next sentence. If a park is missing bridges, the people who visit may fall into the water.

Activity

Draw a literal bridge between the two figures below.

Here are two sentences about the picture above. Circle the sentence pairing that contains the most helpful transition.

1. *There were two stick figures on the page. They were basically the same.*
2. *The two siblings were mostly the same. However, one had a hairstyle that made the other jealous.*

The second sentence contains a helpful transition. You might also form a bridge transition between the two sentences like this:

3. *The two siblings were basically the same. Their similarity ended with hairstyle.*

Note that the repetition of *the same/their similarity* helps to link the two sentences together.

Activity

Below is a list of selected transition words. Look at the list and then complete the activity by adding a transition word or creating a bridge transition between the two sentences.

To Add Information: In addition, Additionally, In the same way

To Show Contrast: However, In contrast, Even though

Examples: In other words, That is to say, For example

Space: In the center, To the left, To the right

Time: First, Second, Third, Later, Formerly

Now create a transition between each of the sentences below.

1. **Original Sentences:** Sometimes violence can be invisible. There are many women and men who suffer from emotional abuse.
2. **Original Sentences:** In our society, children sometimes can't get enough to eat. They can't get enough emotional support.
3. **Original Sentences:** Going to watch a dancing show can provide great emotional relief to you, especially if you are a busy college student. It's not the best idea on the night before a paper you haven't started is due.
4. **Original Sentences:** The first step to writing a successful essay is to decide you want to write it. Get out your computer.
5. **Original Sentences:** The photograph by Cindy Sherman contains a long-faced clown in the center of the composition. There are rainbow colors.
6. **Original Sentences:** There were two orange tabbies. They were basically the same.

Activity

Find pairs of sentences in a paper you have recently written. Create new transitions between each of the sentences. Please note that you may have perfectly excellent transitions between your sentences already, but experimenting with different transitions can really help you to practice different transition strategies that are available to you.

RESEARCH SKILLS

Paraphrasing

People tend to find paraphrasing challenging because it forces you to understand sentences on a very deep level. If you do not understand a sentence fully, you will not be able to paraphrase it accurately. Do not be intimidated! Paraphrasing can be mastered with practice.

Paraphrasing is putting a short amount of text in your own words while still giving proper credit to the author in the form of a citation. There are many ways to do this including looking at a sentence, looking away from the sentence, and magically putting it in your own words! Some people, especially those who have a lot of experience with reading and/or research, do not have to go through individual steps for this process. However, these steps can be very helpful if you are struggling with paraphrasing or if you want to get better at paraphrasing.

Paraphrasing Steps

1. Read the sentence(s) and understand it/them in the context of the article. Then write the sentence down with quotation marks.

2. Do a vocabulary annotation on the sentence (write down the vocabulary words and their definitions).

3. Put the sentence in your own words in your head or out loud to a friend.

4. Change the syntax (order) of your reworded sentence and make sure it still makes sense.

5. Your sentence should be about the same length as the original.

6. Create the citation (Author Page Number).

EXAMPLE:

- *Quotation:* "Community College of Philadelphia should have better athletic equipment," according to Jeb Jones, a student at the college who wrote about the issue in an essay entitled "CCP Needs Work" (4).

- *Paraphrase:* According to Jeb Jones, in an essay called "CCP Needs Work," there could be much improvement in the paraphernalia for sports at the college (4).

What is different about the paraphrased example? Why is there a number four in parentheses?

Activity

1. Select an article that you have read this semester and write down the title and the author.
2. Select a quotation from the article that is at least two consecutive sentences. After the quotation, write the page number following the model on the previous page. Then do a vocabulary annotation on the quotation.
3. Paraphrase, starting with the second sentence and moving to the first. Add a citation to your paraphrase.
4. Read your paraphrase. Does it make sense on its own? Does it mean the same as the original? If not, rewrite it, remembering to still include the citation.

Quotation Sandwich

Have you ever gone to a fast-food restaurant and been given a burger with a bun missing? Hopefully not! What would it be like if you went to a restaurant expecting a full burger and just being handed the meat from the center? First, it might get on your hands and make your hands sticky. It would be hard to eat and probably not taste so good. You would probably ask for your money back. When you are incorporating a quotation into an essay, you also want to make sure that you don't just provide your readers with the meat of your paragraph (the quotation). You have to give the readers something to hold onto to understand your quotation. Below is a method for incorporating quotations into paragraphs.

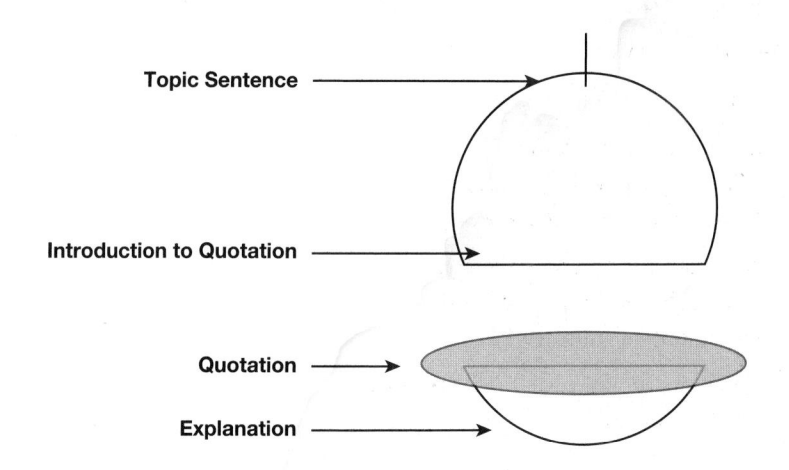

Topic Sentence

Introduction to Quotation

Quotation

Explanation

Quotation: "Community College of Philadelphia should have better athletic equipment like badminton rackets that don't break and fully inflated basketballs" (Jones 4).

Paragraph Incorporating Quotation

One of the ways that Community College of Philadelphia could be improved is to improve various aspects of its athletic program. There are often articles written in the school newspaper about this topic. A recent article by Jeb Jones stated, "Community College of Philadelphia should have better athletic equipment like badminton rackets that don't break and fully inflated basketballs" (4). I agree with Jones that the school should purchase better athletic equipment. The other day, I went to the athletic center and a badminton racket broke while I was playing. One way that the school could get money for better equipment would be to have a raffle after graduation.

Activity

1. Highlight each of the hamburger labels in a different color and then highlight the sample paragraph with corresponding colors. For example, you could highlight the topic sentence next to the hamburger in pink and highlight the topic sentence of the paragraph in pink.
2. Write down a quotation with citation.
3. Practice putting that quotation in a quotation sandwich paragraph following the example above.

17

ACTIVITIES FOR IMPROVING YOUR WRITING

REVISION ACTIVITY

1. Write about the process of writing your last essay. What did you do first, second, third, and so on?
2. Write about any academic challenges you had writing your last essay.
3. Write about any emotional challenges you had writing your last essay (e.g., procrastination).
4. What do you want to make sure you do next time regarding your essay process?
5. What do you want to make sure you don't do next time regarding your essay process?
6. Based on your instructor's feedback, what are three specific skills you are going to work on before you write your next essay? For example: *I am going to reread my essay a third time to look for run-on sentences and sentence fragments. I will make sure that I add three more specific details than last time. I will write a longer conclusion.*

PEER REVIEW ACTIVITY

First read your partner's essay. Then answer the following questions.

1. Review the possible structure for your partner's essay. Below, write down at least three sentences that follow the essay structure. Label these sentences with their names. Some examples include topic sentences, thesis statements, introduction, and so on.
2. Write down the most specific or precise moment in the essay and explain whether or not it is effective.
3. Write down a sentence where vocabulary is being used well in the essay.
4. If you feel comfortable, offer two specific critiques of your partner's writing. Please do not offer critiques in areas where you most struggle. For example, if you routinely make sentence boundary errors, focus instead on offering suggestions in essay structure (if you have had success in essay structure).
5. Discuss your answers with your partner. Then write down what you learned from reading your partner's essay.

THESIS STATEMENT ACTIVITY

This activity can be done with fellow classmates inside or outside of the classroom. Follow the steps below to write a compelling and effective thesis statement.

1. On an index card or piece of paper, write down the thesis statement for whatever essay you are working on, following the guidelines you were given in class or the guidelines in your textbook.
2. Get at least four people to stand at the front of the room, and read your thesis statement to them.
3. If they agree with your thesis statement they should move to the right and if they disagree with it they should move to the left. If they are confused or neutral, they should stand in the middle.
4. Ask the people at the front questions about why they are standing where they are standing and take notes.

If there are a lot of people in the middle, your thesis statement may not be arguable enough. Some people may be confused by your thesis statement and also be in the middle. If everyone is agreeing, consider your audience. Is your audience people who already agree with you? Do you want this? If everyone disagrees, make a note that you have to convince your audience. If the people in the front of the room give examples for their perspectives, write them down to potentially use (with attribution) or refute as needed. Feel free to switch roles after you have gotten the notes you need.

TOPIC SENTENCES ACTIVITY

Depending on the type of essay you are writing, the topic sentences can be very different. Here is an activity to help you with essays that are less analytical and contain more narrative elements.

Highlight the topic sentences and tell how you know that they are the topic sentences.

1. Here is an overview of a place that's significant to my life: Atlantic City. Atlantic City is in New Jersey. It takes two hours to get there. It has go-carts and an art cave. The beach is nice and relaxing. The water is very cold; it has shells in the water. Atlantic City is always crowded. The restaurants are good. My family and I go there every summer. We always walk the boardwalk, which is very long. There are many opportunities to have fun with your family in Atlantic City!

2. My family and I have a lot of memories there. My mom gets free rooms so we always stay at the Four Seasons or Bally's hotel. One time when we were at Four Seasons, my brothers and I took a four-hour-long walk on the beach at 7 a.m. This was a great memory because usually we do not like each other, but this time we really bonded. In addition, I remember going to the all-you-can-eat buffet and trying crab legs for the first time when I was very young while in Atlantic City. I would like to continue to make memories there.

USING MODELS ACTIVITY

Follow the steps below to look deeply at a piece of writing that is the same as your piece of writing.

1. Write down the type of writing that you are working on here. For example, research study, argument, persuasive essay, and so on.

2. Find an essay that is in the genre you are writing. Use your writing textbook to find the article or go online to your library database. You might have a sample from your teacher or even use a successful sample student essay provided by your teacher. Below is a selected list of websites that you can use to find articles in the genre that you may be writing if you do not have access to these sources. Note, find these sources by going into a search engine and typing in both the genre and the source (e.g., feature story, *The New York Times*). If the type of article you are writing is not listed below, type the genre with the word "example" into a search engine or ask your instructor or fellow classmate for ideas.

    a. Feature Story—*The New York Times* or *The Guardian* online
    b. Research Report—*Rockefeller Archive Center*

    c. Infographic—*Wired*

    d. Causal Analysis—*Science Direct*

    e. Research Study—*Psychology Today*

    f. Flow Diagram—*Google*

    g. Argument—*Washington Post* Op-Ed Section

3. Decide how you want to work with the article. The instructions below will ask you to highlight/copy down information, so if you have access to a printer or copy machine, that might be a good strategy. You might also write down the information for the following questions in your notebook or in a document on a computer.

4. What is the title of the piece? Does the title make clear the genre of the piece? What about the title might inspire a title for your piece or a revision of your current title?

5. Does this piece contain a thesis statement? If so, what is it and where is it located? Is the thesis statement direct or implied? Is the thesis statement or lack of thesis statement consistent with what you learned about this genre of writing?

6. Copy down or highlight the first sentence of the first three paragraphs in this essay (excluding the introductory paragraph). Do these sentences convey the overall point of the paragraphs or do they serve a different function? What can you learn from them?

7. Write down two supporting details in this essay. Do the supporting details tend to be personal examples, statistics, or quotations from other sources? All of the above? Make a comment about how these points are balanced in the article. Are all personal examples in one paragraph and all statistics in another? Is there a blend of information?

8. Write down three vocabulary words in this piece of writing. How might you use them in your writing?

9. What is contained in the conclusion of this essay? How is it structured?

10. What do you find to be successful about the content of the article (the overall points the article is making)?

11. What do you find to be successful about the structure and rhetorical strategies of the article (how it was written)? What strategies would you like to use in your paper or in a revision of your paper?